WORKING IN SERIES

CHRISTOPHER C. M. LEE AND KAPIL GUPTA / SERIE ARCHITECTS

Architectural Association London

CONTENTS

CEILING / VAULTS

PLAN / CIRCLES

FACADE / GRIDS

GOING AGAINST TYPE

AN INTRODUCTION TO SERIE

Brett Steele

The work of Serie renews one of the decisive critical projects of architectural theory and practice from the 1960s and 1970s: that of type and typology. To say the least, this renewal is something of a surprise, especially given the rapid decline of typological discourse amidst the worst excesses of 1980s historicist post-modernism. Serie reject the cultural nostalgia exhibited by so many of their generational peers in relation to architectural history (and, with it, the frequent prioritising of appearance over form). And they have none of the digital determinism of today's parametricists, who assert that scripted, relational design platforms are the only legitimate basis for arguing correct architectural form. Instead, they seek something else entirely: to pursue architecture through the renewal of already known disciplinary or critical projects.

Serie's contemporary insight owes much to their intelligent combining of the most advanced design platforms with a decidedly self-aware understanding of recent architectural culture: they have realised that no other recurring modern project within architecture has a greater capacity to renovate design theories than architectural typology, with its focus on the inherently iterative, serial aspects of architectural production itself. On the surface, such an assertion goes against the grain of our era's fascination with mass-customisation and nearly infinite cross-disciplinary collaborations, which leave little room for historical or typological precedent.

Over the past 15 years, architecture has lost much of the historical knowledge by which it formerly understood not just itself, but the whole world around it. Architecture's greatest forms of knowledge and expertise have always been those related to its own disciplinary history. For 2,000 years, from the *Ten Books* of Vitruvius, historical knowledge was embedded within a decidedly iterative and serial embodiment of architectural design. By early modern times, this had become codified in treatises describing formal architectural typologies of all kinds, from the arrangement of institutional structures to the proportioning of walls and decorative elements.

The revolutions related to early 20th-century modernism were founded, of course, on an outright antagonism to all of this, and most especially to historical strategies for the organisation of buildings. Centuries of disciplinary intelligence were stripped from the design language, tools and rhetoric of architecture and replaced with a surreal range of functionalist accounts of all kinds, which sought to validate modern architectural form.

It was against this historical backdrop that the architectural interest in typology was rekindled in the writings of the late-modern generation, most notably by Aldo Rossi in his 1966 *Architettura della città*. Rossi's text offered a generational corrective to the excesses of architectural orthodoxy, which by the middle years of the 20th century had become entrenched and virtually incapable of expressing contextual, let alone historical, coherence between modern architecture and the city. Rossi argued that building typologies possessed a unique capacity for creating such coherence: what is more, they achieved this through an act of iteration, not reproduction, which allowed architecture to understand itself (and *not* just the city) as a *historical* reality. This conceptual breakthrough within modernism was huge, if short-lived.

Throughout the 1970s the writings of Rossi and others on typology ended up being morphed into various kinds of contextualism that sought above all a justifiable fit between architectural form and its real (or imagined) historical setting – a condition that quickly devolved into a weakened architectural historicism. However, 1978 saw the publication of two genuine manifestos that pointed to the productive relevance of typological thinking. *Collage City*, by Colin Rowe and Fred Koetter, pursued a typological assessment of the classical versus the modernist city along a traditional, planimetric form of analysis focusing on Nolli's Rome and Le Corbusier's Paris. Rem Koolhaas's *Delirious New York*, on the other hand, presented a deeply typological assessment of modernism in the form of a distinctive sectional reading of the generic urban block comprising the Manhattan grid. While differing in significant and contrasting ways, both texts demonstrated the considerable instrumental capacity of typology to serve as the basis for architectural experimentation.

But what has changed since the writing of these texts, and what makes a return of critical theories of type and typology so unexpected today, is the definitive globalisation of architectural culture during the past three decades. (Indeed, one might say that by the 90s Koolhaas's critical interest in the brute realities of globalisation, like the generic plan or 'bigness', testified to his generation's loss of faith in older, historical/critical architectural projects.) Chris Lee, Kapil Gupta and their young collaborators at Serie work out of offices in London, Mumbai, Beijing and Chengdu, demonstrating in the most straightforward way the spectacular global working realities of the generation of architects coming of age today.

This book could also be seen as both a testament to and effect of this condition, documenting a substantial body of work achieved barely three years after the founding of this young practice – something that could scarcely be imagined without the kinds of distributed, networked and collaborative practices that Serie have so clearly embraced. What is clear, however, is that this reality is no longer seen as a subject for sustained reflection, but is instead treated as merely a working condition around which larger, genuinely disciplinary, architectural interests are pursued.

The work of Serie is an attempt to renew architecture's legitimacy through a retrieval of the working concepts, language and history of architectural serialism, that is, through the recognition that an architectural project is only ever the latest in a series of similar undertakings – either in one's career, or in the history of the profession more generally. To a remarkable degree architectural knowledge is only ever learned one project at a time: this blunt (and for many architects, brutal) condition of architectural life is something Serie are well aware of, to the point that their projects are compelling not only for their formal accomplishment but also for the various ways in which they talk to one another, as iterations or minor deviations of shared design operations or techniques. Add to this level of self-awareness the fact that so many of the projects are themselves the result of complex organisations based upon the repetition of simple, primary shapes (circles, slabs, openings) or formal operations (rotating, branching, tiling), and what becomes obvious is that this is the work of young architects who are interested not only in redefining architectural types but in architectural form itself, pursued here via various kinds of iteration, seriality and differentiation. That these design operations are exactly those iterative actions biased by scriptable, controllable digital design software demonstrates the larger potential of Serie's renewal of type and typology. The promise that history and technology might yet again productively co-exist within the culture of contemporary experimental architecture is exactly what is suggested by this early work. Serie are believers in architecture's own and distinctive ability to transform itself – not once and forever, but over and over, in a world where architecture is best understood as a serial form of knowledge, experience and ambition.

Far from rules being injurious to invention, it must be said that invention does not exist outside rules; for there would be no way to judge invention. – Quatremère de Quincy

Architecture is an artistic and not a scientific discipline. Architectural activity has its own object of knowledge, which is different from the object of science. The object of architectural knowledge is architecture itself, as it has been historically constituted. It does not consist of abstract functions but of concrete forms. – Alan Colquhoun

WORKING IN SERIES
TOWARDS AN OPERATIVE THEORY OF TYPE

Christopher C. M. Lee

What is the common currency of architecture in the post-Fordist city? And what is the disciplinary knowledge that enables the effective production and comprehension of architecture in a globalised world?

It can be argued that globalisation is not a new phenomenon but it cannot be denied that the rate of space–time compression has increased rapidly in the past two decades, affecting the nature of architectural production in the context of the city and raising the above questions.[1] To illustrate the point: I was born in Malaysia, of Chinese origin, a British citizen, living in London. I teach at the AA – arguably the most international school of architecture. My partner, Kapil Gupta, is Indian, based in Mumbai and we founded Serie London/ Mumbai three years ago. Serie now has offices in London, Mumbai, Beijing and Chengdu and our projects are spread across Xi'an, Hangzhou, Beijing, Chengdu, London, Bratislava and Mumbai. Unlike offices that have amassed a large portfolio and a clear 'style' prior to expansion, our practice was global from the start, in very modest and local settings. With time differences, distance and cultural, political and social nuances as obstacles, the most pressing issue from the outset was the need for an operative theory that would not only create a basis for a consistent body of work but also enable the practice to engage in the varied cultures and locations. This operative theory, I believe, should fall within architecture's disciplinary knowledge and should be a generic knowledge – to sustain comprehension across the various offices, time zones and cultures – but must also be capable of offering very specific and explicit architectural responses. The processes adopted have to be logical in experimentation rather than personal.

1   David Harvey, *The Condition of Postmodernity: An Enquiry into the Origins of Cultural Change* (Blackwell, 1990)

4

For me, this operative theory is *type* – albeit an understanding of type and typology that has to be renewed. Thus the work of Serie revolves around the notion of type as an operative theory and a disciplinary knowledge that transcends national and cultural borders and is dedicated to the search of dominant types, both as ideas and models that are simultaneously generic enough to overcome differences and specific enough to engage and index the cultural, social and political nuances of its host. At the core, it is an attempt to enable architecture to regain a certain degree of political agency in an age of pluralism.

TYPE AS IDEA AND MODEL

The concept of type was formally introduced into architectural theory by Quatremère de Quincy in the early nineteenth century. For de Quincy 'The word type presents less the image of a thing to copy or imitate completely than the idea of an element which ought itself to serve as a rule for the model'.[2] For Quatremère, type is an element, an object, a thing, that embodies the idea. Type is abstract and conceptual rather than concrete and literal. Drawing upon Plato's theory of art, he goes on to define this notion of idea more as an ideal, and this idea – that must serve as the rule to the model – compels the creative process to imitate the idea and to strive for the ideal.[3] Thus, working from type involves the process of reasoning and abstraction. The model, on the other hand, is concrete and is the complete thing.[4] Stressing this difference warns against the biggest pitfall of using type in the design process: namely, that an over reliance on precedent leads to repetition and direct copying and excludes originality and invention. Therefore, if the type is an idea, its material

manifestation and expression can take on many different forms. Thinking through type allows the architect to reach the essence of the element in question, rather than using it as a model to be copied. This affirmation for the *idea* draws attention to type as a primarily cultural and aesthetic construct. It is abstract and constitutes a form of critical reasoning.

The *model* on the other hand can be traced, almost at the same time, to the way Durand treats the notion of type and has been commonly associated more to typology as a design method. In his *Précis*, Durand attempts to find a systematic method to classify various genres of buildings and to distil them in a set of diagrams.[5] Durand proposes that new types for the recently emerging urban condition can be created through the adaptation of these diagrams to specific sites, responding to its constraints. It can be argued that the danger of Durand's process of abstraction reduces building precedents to a set of geometric diagrams and removes from type the very idea proposed by Quatremère. Nevertheless, the notion of type as model, represented graphically as diagrams, introduces precepts that are fundamental to working typologically: precedents, classification, taxonomy, continuity, repetition, differentiation and reinvention. Although the process begins with a precedent type, the fundamental goal of working typologically is to surpass the precedent type whilst maintaining its irreducible traits or DNA in the transformed or reinvented type. Taken together with Quatremère's notion of type, this continuity between past and present, norm and exception, allows the practice of architecture to locate its role in the discursive formation of the knowledge and history of architecture. Seen this way, to work typologically is to analyse, reason and propose through things which are of the same type, thus considering them in series. Working in series allows us to understand the shared traits between things – be it architecture or the city – and to harness the embodied and cumulative intelligence of that series into architectural projections. Furthermore, this serial consideration emancipates the idea of type from a fixed ideal without displacing the need for an ideal. As Argan has pointed out, 'The birth of a "type" is therefore dependent on the existence of a series

---

2   Quatremère de Quincy, 'Type' in *Encyclopédie Méthodique*, vol. 3, trans. Samir Younés, reprinted in *The Historical Dictionary of Architecture of Quatremère de Quincy* (Papadakis Publisher, 2000).

3   Consistent with the discourse of art and architecture from the mid eighteenth to mid nineteenth century that delves into the question of architecture's origin, as exemplified by Laugier's primitive hut, Quatremère de Quincy takes nature's laws and principles as the ideal and urges architects to be the artificers of nature.

4   Quatremère de Quincy elaborates further the difference between type and model with the following statement: 'The model, understood in the sense of practical execution, is an object that should be repeated as it is; contrariwise, the type is an object after which each artist can conceive works that bear no resemblance to each other. All is precise and given when it comes to the model, while all is more or less vague when it comes to the type.'

5   Jean Nicolas Louis Durand, *Précis of the Lectures on Architecture*, trans. David Britt (Getty, 2000). Durand's diagrams primarily capture the structural elements of various building types, comprising a layer of grids that denotes both structure and geometric composition.

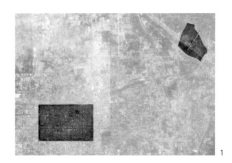

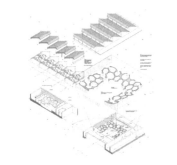

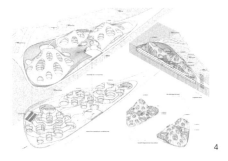

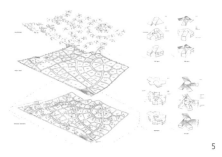

of buildings having between them an obvious formal and functional analogy'.[6] This assertion also leads to the crucial fact that new types can be detected as much as they can be surpassed, hence enabling a design process that is syntactic and discursive in equal measure.

Central to this proposed operative theory of type is the utilisation of the diagram. As Jeffrey Kipnis succinctly writes, 'diagrams underwrite all typological theories, as evidenced, for example, in the catalogues of Durand'.[7] Ever since the utilisation of the diagram, from the bubble to syntactic formalism and the all pervasive parametric indexicality today affirms its continued instrumentality in architectural experimentation. It can be argued that this indexical obsession in academia and in some speculative practices for the past two decades draws from the same ambition to institute the rigorous system of architectural knowledge afforded by the diagram. However, the focus for this continued obsession has largely been around the generation of novel form – with today's latest incarnation of parametric design. It would be far too exhaustive to cover the various differences above in this essay but it is sufficient to state that for Serie the diagram and its processes serve to carry the typal imprints of a precedent type and to evolve them into new configurations that will form a series of possibilities. The utilisation of the diagram and the notion of type as a model is well equipped to answer the question 'how to …' but is inadequate in the face of the question 'why do…'. It is therefore the coupling of the notion of type as idea through Quatremère with that of the model that will enable architectural experimentation to address both its internal disciplinary problem and its wider existential question. The idea here for us is the critical reasoning of type tied to cultural, social and political considerations. The domain where these considerations are manifested in all their material complexity, as tangible architecture, is the city itself. The city as the artefact and repository of civilisation enables us to understand – through its dominant types – our cultural, social and political struggles. The ideas of our architecture are driven largely by the idea of the city and, where possible, our ambition is to produce architecture that is relevant for the city.

6   Giulio Carlo Argan, 'On the Typology of Architecture', trans Joseph Rykwert in *Architectural Design* no. 33 (December. 1963): 564–65.
7   Jeffrey Kipnis, 'Re-originating Diagrams' in *Peter Eisenman Feints* (Skira, 2006).

TYPOLOGICAL CONFLICT AND CONCEIT

We begin each project in our office by locating a typological conflict. This contention articulates Quatremère's notion of type as 'the idea that must serve as the rule to the model' – the intellection of the project towards action. This typological conflict is often exposed and conceptualised through the dialectical organisation that structures the complexity of contemporary relations. From the programmatic organisation of rooms to the dispersion of architectural artefacts in the city, typological conflicts embody the different conflicting interests that are constantly renegotiated in the contemporary conditions of heterogeneity. This analysis and reasoning attempt to go beyond the demands of a design brief that a service professional will diligently meet and push the practice of architecture into a conjectural discipline. For instance, our Xi'an Horticultural Expo proposal was at odds with the brief that called for the sprinkling of 'ornamental' greenhouses in a newly proposed park and instead submitted the idea that a large architectural artefact was needed to form a new focus at the periphery of the city – anchoring its future growth and countering the ancient city wall at the centre of the historical city (figs 1 & 2). The formulation of an alternative agenda, beyond the given parameters and confines set out by a client brief can be seen as an act of resistance to the banal forces of the market. However, this position of resistance does not seek to negate the reality of practice but attempts to carve out a position of autonomy for alternative projections and meaningful alternatives within the same milieu.[8] In this way, the internal discourse of architecture's disciplinary knowledge acquires a political agency through its direct engagement with the forces external to its concerns.

THE DEEP STRUCTURE OF TYPE

Architecture in practice cannot remain as a form of critique. The *idea* of type – the reasoning that governs the principles of the proposition – requires the *model* as the concrete abstraction of that principle. The model, unlike the idea, can be graphically represented as the deep structure of the type. This deep structure can be best understood in two ways. Firstly, the deep structure is the diagram that indexes the typal imprint of the precedent type. Secondly, the deep structure is the irreducible structure that gives rise to organisation. The unity of organisation and structure is where form, tectonics, construction and materiality cohere into the aforementioned typal imprint. At this juncture, type is pre-architecture and exists as a diagram of pure serial potential. The projects developed by Serie so far can be classified into three groups of deep structures, each exploring an irreducible typal imprint and are paired up with a corresponding orthographic plane of exploration that gives rise to the following: plan/circles, facade/grids and ceiling/vaults. The diagrammatic approach adopted here as a process of abstraction is not to search for novel geometries or form – common in the practice of interpretation of the graphic space of convoluted diagrams. Instead, type as a diagram is both a diagnostic and prognostic tool, an index of organisational and structural performance that carries a specific idea or strategy. In many instances, the deep structure is trans-scalar and independent of building use – evidenced in the Blue Frog Acoustic Lounge, Parcel 9 HX Urban Centre and Boháčky Masterplan (figs 3, 4 & 5) – providing a consistency in organisation and an open system.

The recent retreat of academia and speculative architectural practices from the problem of organisation as the agency where architecture can exert influence on how spaces are contested, negotiated and consensually settled is unfortunate. This retreat in favour of the obsession with the figure of the building (icon) and the *faciality* of the skin of the building (envelope) further reduces the territory of influence for the practice of architecture – the former whimsically forces organisation into a figured envelope, turning architects into building stylists and the latter relinquishes organisation altogether to developers, space planners, retail specialists or building service consultants and focuses solely on the proliferation of components on the envelope. In contrast, architecture as a practice has at its disposal the disciplinary knowledge to deploy organisational intelligence that can fundamentally engage the complexity of spatial relations between disparate user groups, the natural and artificial environment, the urban fabric and its building mass – conditions that typify the disorienting heterogeneous environments

---

8   Pier Vittorio Aureli, *The Project of Autonomy: Politics and Architecture within and against Capitalism* (Temple Hoyne Buell Center for the Study of American Architecture, 2008). The argument set forth by Aureli centres around the possibility of a critical architecture that is propositional and projective by revisiting the theoretical positions and projects of Aldo Rossi and Archizoom through the lens of the autonomia movement and its thinkers like Mario Tronti.

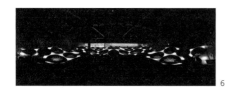

6

7

8

9

10

as a result of space–time compression.[9] Organisational structures – or in Le Corbusier's digitally unassisted times, the plan – is the generator of other inventions in architecture. It is this that gives rise to other formal variations, the *Plan Libre* (organisation) and Domino House (structure) that enabled the free facade (surface/envelope). The same could be said of the Assembly Building in Chandigarh, where the organisation of the figured function in plan eliminated the container–content relationship thus freeing the facade for experimentation. Thus Le Corbusier's *brise-soleil* – as an invention – was perhaps inspired by the freedom afforded by a new organisational structure first and foremost, rather than by the need for a considered climatic response.[10]

We learn from Rossi that type is ultimately independent of programmatic failure.[11] That is to say, the deep structure of type – its organisational structures – is not genre or programme specific and as such is open to scalar shifts. This is evident in most projects of OMA; take for instance the Y2K House and Casa da Musica, Porto. The former is a house, the latter a concert hall, but both share the same organisational structure and form and are thus of the same type. Both projects carry the idea of exhibiting the concealed spaces of social intercourse and the model enables this through the framing of the void (the family room of the Y2K House and the performance hall for Casa da Musica) and projecting the void to the exterior, heightening the tension between exhibitionism and voyeurism. This transcalar programmatic immunity is evident in all our projects. One such series utilises the circle as a figure and organisation, giving rise to a range of typological possibilities: an undulated lounge and restaurant that behaves like a theatre (void as stalls), the vernacular Hakka Tulou House recast and framed within an undulating landscape (void as courtyards) and the plot boundaries as an undulating regulator of difference (void as regulators of intensive difference), (figs 6, 7, & 8). In another series, the explorations of the ceiling – an often undervalued architectural element and plane for design – as a volumetric definer finds its expression in the structural paraboloid vaults that are part wall, part bridge and part greenhouse in the

9   David Harvey, *The Condition of Postmodernity: An Enquiry into the Origins of Cultural Change* (Blackwell, 1990).
10   Alejandro Zaera Polo, 'The Politics of the Envelope', *Volume 17*, 88.
11   Aldo Rossi, *The Architecture of the City* (MIT Press, 1984).

11

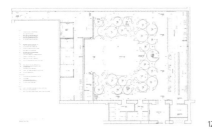

12

13

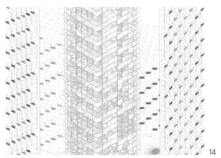

14

Xi'an Horticultural Expo Masterplan (fig 9). The ceiling as the primary volumetric definer is articulated by the branching structure in The Tote, whereby a secondary volume is created within an outdoor volume, enveloped by the site's majestic rain trees. In the Meswani House, intersecting vaults enable the loose arrangement of a very large house, eliminating long corridors in favour of punctuated light wells and courtyards as circulation rooms (fig 10).

Organisational structures as the deep structure of type offer the required pliability to engage with the specific and increasingly complex and heterogeneous demands of contemporary life. The demands are often contradictory and are reflected in the impossible briefs that architects work with – a big house that must be compact and intimate (Meswani House, fig 11), an old factory that must now house a restaurant, bar, lounge, dance floor and performance space in one and the same volume (Blue Frog Acoustic Lounge, fig 12); a disused factory that must be conserved, made prominent again and yet accommodate a new insertion of built floor area four times its existing footprint (Xin Tian Di Factory H, fig 13).

The grids in the Ružinov Middle Income Housing and V-Office projects are utilised not only for the demonstration of part to whole harmony but for the seeding of differentiated organisation behind a regular facade. In Ružinov, a project that calls for the construction of low cost apartments, the placement of projecting loggias in a 1:2 bay forces the displacement of the living room of apartments along the loggias. This facade completely disables the stacking of identical apartments and as a result generates 56 unique apartment layouts (fig 14). Despite the high degree of customisation of the layouts (at no considerable increase in cost), the deep structure of the facade/ grids achieves two aims. The first denies the rampant random facades that typify mass housing of late, where the conspicuous expression of different apartment units on the facade as singular instances (and as a celebration of individuality) denies any sense of order and coherence and negates the very notion of collective housing. Following on from this, the second aim is to provide for a high degree of differentiation in apartment layouts where these differences cohere into a collective whole that is ordered and legible.

IDEAS FROM AND FOR THE CITY

Our interest in the city as the overt site for architectural knowledge is more evident in our recent larger projects, namely the Boháčky Residential Masterplan, Xi'an Horticultural Expo Masterplan, Parcel 9, Guiyang and Xin Tian Di Factory H. This proposition that the city is the domain of critical reasoning leading towards typological ideas is based on our realisation that the dominant type embodies the idea of the city. From Cerda's housing blocks in Barcelona, Georgian and Victorian terraces in London to the skyscrapers of Manhattan, cities can be understood, described, conceptualised and theorised through their own peculiar dominant types. Through Rossi, we learn that a singular building as an element of 'permanence' is able to act as the repository of a city's history, construction and form within its type. For Rossi, type is independent of function and therefore pliable, as the city's repository.[12] Thus, to understand these types is to understand the city itself. This possibility of conceptualising and theorising a city through a singular dominant type also led Koolhaas to mythologise the idea of Manhattan as the culture of congestion – all embodied within the Downtown Athletic Club.[13] Here, the skyscraper is recast as the apotheosis of metropolitan culture, a building type made up of a stack of autonomous, richly varied programmes coexisting in a singular tower, made possible by the introduction of the elevator. Today, the reliance on a singular type to envision and brand new cities is evident in the iconic high-rises of Dubai and Shanghai. Here, type is no longer utilised or valued as a formative element of the city but is deployed to lubricate the marketing machinery of capitalism, where novelty and excess is the prerequisite for a city's global status. Thus, the idea of the city finds its ultimate expression in the dominant type.

What is revealing about the architects who wrote about the city from 1966 to 1978 – namely Rossi in *The Architecture of the City,* Venturi, Scott Brown & Izenour in *Learning from Las Vegas* and Koolhaas in *Delirious New York* – is that they went on to produce more significant buildings than masterplans and that the city is treated not so much as a site that must be transformed by masterplans or propositions of similar scale after the initial readings, but most crucially as an idea for a projective architecture. Thus, the ideas of the city, once conceptualised, can be abstracted and transposed as architectural ideas. This is evident in Rossi's seminal works, the Gallaratese housing and Modena Cemetery, where the idea of architecture is understood through a singular architectural artefact. That is to say, the *dominant type* is and can still be a mnemonic structure for the city. Similarly, the defining section of the Downtown Athletic Club became the didactic diagram for Koolhaas' subsequent projects where the traditional clarity of the figure/ground and building/city idea is recast as an architectural idea based on the denial of the ground. In these projects, the neat divisions between functional zoning, site and building, ground, solids and voids, are dismantled to conjure up the culture of congestion.[14] Similarly, emerging cities today offer us many fertile ideas to rethink normative architectural ideas. It might be the possibility that a single dominant type as a punctuator, independent of intended programmatic effectiveness could regenerate a city through excessive novelty and contextual contrast, as in the case of Gehry's Guggenheim in Bilbao; or, in the example of the airport as a type, where it has mutated and expanded to a city in its own right. The Aerotropolis offers, among many others, an idea of architecture as a new type of mat building, a type with extreme flatness and depth of programmatic diversity – a hyper-large architecture as a city.

Our proposal for the Xi'an Horticultural Expo Masterplan is perhaps the clearest attempt to draw upon the proposition outlined above. Going beyond the brief for a cluster of dispersed greenhouses, exhibition and performance halls and other associative amenities, our proposal attempts to rethink the idea of centrality on the periphery of cities. Learning from the ancient city wall of Xi'an, the clear figure of

12   Rossi's idea of the city rests in his assertion that the city can and should be understood through its architecture as a whole and that the city is a gigantic cumulative construction over time, embodying its history and memory. He cites Palazzo della Ragione in Padua as an example of an architectural artefact of 'permanence', able to absorb different uses through time. This suggests that its deep structure (structural elements that give rise to organisation) is independent of function and is an element of permanence in the city. This reading of the city enabled Rossi to use the fragments of historical urban archetypes as set pieces for a present context, denying a linear and singular historical narrative, yet maintaining an ambiguous continuity with the historical city. See 'The Structure of Urban Artefacts',ibid.

13   Rem Koolhaas, *Delirious New York* (010, 1994). See also Eisenman's description of the instrumentality of the Downtown Athletic Club as a didactic diagram for the subsequent OMA projects of the Bibliothèque de France, Agadir Convention Centre, Jussieu Library and Seattle Public Library in Peter Eisenman, *Ten Canonical Buildings: 1950 – 2000* (Rizzoli, 2008)

14   Ibid, 200–08.

15

the fortified city wall still persists today as the quintessential architectural element that anchors the entire city and forms the city core despite the city's growth beyond its metropolitan border. This figure as a diagram of power and organisation suggested the necessity of centrality to anchor any new growth on the city's northeast periphery where the competition site is located (fig 1). Our proposal re-imagines the city wall as a 1 km-long wall and bridge that houses five climate zones. Each climate zone is experienced sequentially as different episodes of greenhouses strung between the existing historical city and the growth of a future city at its periphery.

Similarly, the utilisation of an inhabited plinth as a podium to accentuate a disused factory in the Xin Tian Di Factory H introduces the idea of a punctuator as a strategy to anchor a masterplan. This idea rests on the possibility that a new urban core can be anchored by a clear and defined artefact rather than the common strategy of utilising hyperdense buildings that accumulate pedestrian flow. The use of the plinth here absorbs the required new floor area for the project but releases the void of the factory hall relatively unmolested by the increase in floor areas, thus turning this large and unique void into a new public space and attractor for the masterplan (fig 15).

The Boháčky Residential Masterplan was an opportunity for us to rethink the question of coherence and difference in a large-scale development. In this masterplan, intended to guide the development of a number of villas by eight other architects, our first concern was to avoid an architectural theme park for designers. Our proposal uses two regulating strategies to achieve a condition of unified plurality: the first strategy utilises an undulating hedge that acts as a green 'wall' that delineates each plot as 'rooms' (fig 16). The second strategy relies on the use of the courtyard type that offers wide multiple variations of pin-wheeled rooms and establishes a typological grammar for other architects (fig 17). In the process, our project rethinks the boundaries as walls that frame individuated difference whilst offering an overall coherence.

To summarise, the idea of the city – with all its antecedent intellections – and the idea of architecture are interchangeable and transposable if the city is understood and conceptualised through its dominant type. It is a given that the contemporary city is an increasingly heterogeneous environment, and its ability to accommodate multiple and

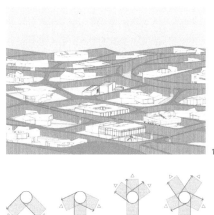

16

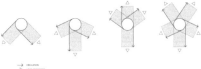

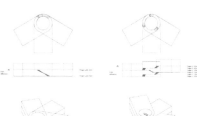

17

often conflicting demands is fundamental. It is this accommodation of differences (as opposed to producing novel forms for the sake of difference), that the deep structure as an organisational framework as well as a common grammar for the multitude can lend architectural propositions and conjectures a degree relevance. This operative theory that works serially through the idea and model – critically confronting the received principles that underwrite the architectural act and harnessing the cumulative intelligence of the type in question – revalorises the practice of architecture as a speculative discipline with a political agency. And it is this constant engagement through the disciplinary knowledge of architecture, via type, that will enable architects to ultimately answer the question 'why architecture?'

DEEP STRUCTURE 1

CEILING / VAULTS

The Tote, Mumbai

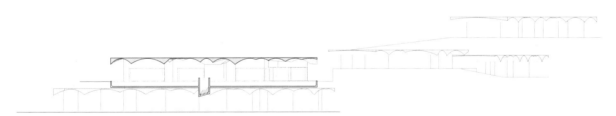

Meswani House, Pavna

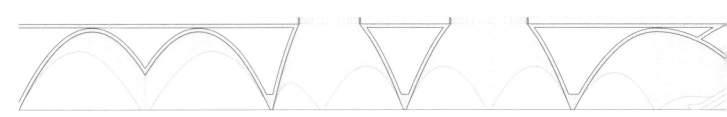

Xi'an 2011 International Horticultural Expo Masterplan, Xi'an

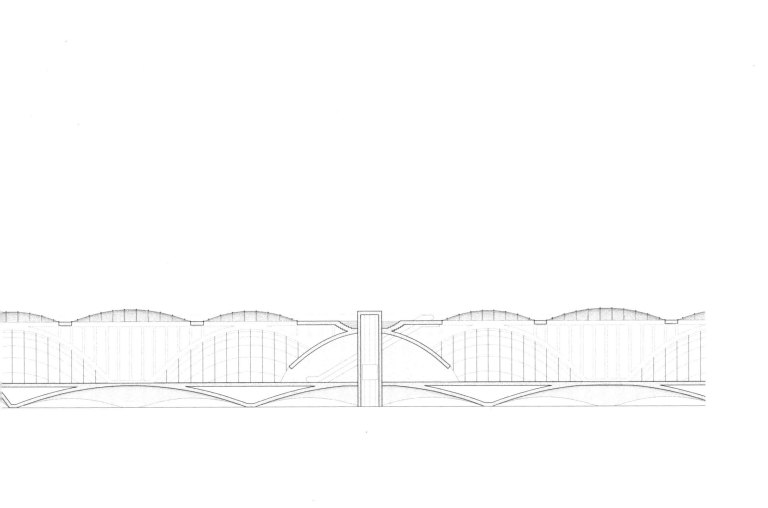

THE TOTE
2007–09, MUMBAI, INDIA

Being primarily a conservation and adaptive re-use project, the challenge of The Tote was two-fold. The first was to avoid the recreation of the historical image of the project and the treatment of the precedent type as an idealised image of an imagined past. The second was to utilise a deep structure that could nevertheless situate the project in this particular setting.

The design brief for The Tote called for the conversion of a series of disused buildings within the Mumbai Racecourse into a banqueting hall, restaurant and bar. The conservation guidelines required the preservation of the roof profile for three-quarters of the buildings and full conservation for the remaining quarter.

The interesting aspect of the site, however, lies not in these colonial buildings but in the open spaces covered by mature rain trees. These spaces are shaded throughout the year by the trees' large leaves, allowing almost the entire programme to occur outdoors. Our proposal attempts to continue this idea of a continuously differentiated space, with no clear boundary, into the envelope of the conservation building.

We proposed a new structure within the old building envelope that would articulate a series of arches that in turn would induce a vaulted ceiling. This articulated ceiling as implied vaults would then act as programmatic captures, defining appropriate volumes under the conservation envelope. The deep structure adopted here is that of a branching-structure, acting both as a volumetric definer and structure to hold up the roof. The progeny of the branching structure along the longitudinal section of the conserved building is differentiated in its growth along the transverse section. This reorganises the old buildings with new dining programmes. Therefore each dining programme (wine bar, restaurant, pre-function and banquet facilities) is captured within a different spatial volume, defined by the variable degree of the branching structure. The structure branches into finer structural members as it approaches the ceiling. When the branches touch the ceiling, the ceiling plane is punctured with a series of openings corresponding to the intersection of the branches with the purlins and rafters. These openings become light coves and slits.

As a whole, the project attempts to bring together the spaces that are already defined by the trees and spaces within the envelope of the building, not through the direct copying of nature, but as Quatremère de Quincy puts it, to imitate the principles that govern the working of nature.

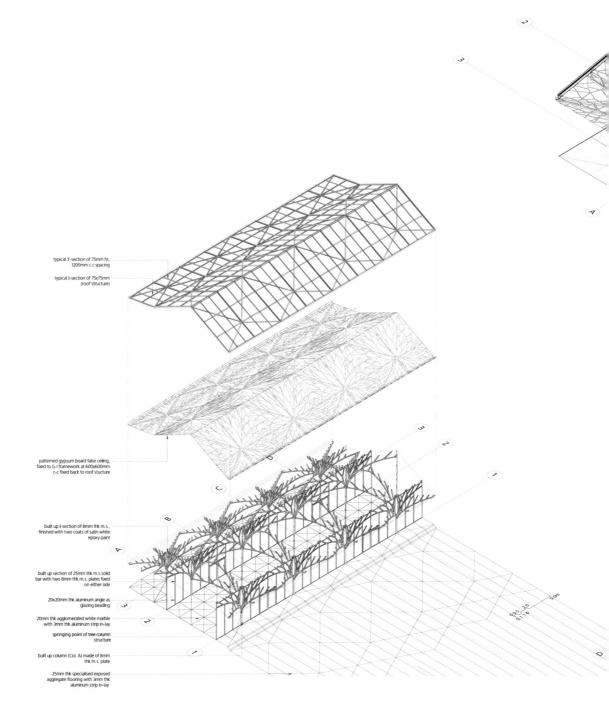

typical T-section of 75mm ht,
1200mm c.c spacing

typical I-section of 75x75mm
(roof structure)

patterned gypsum board false ceiling,
fixed to G.I framework at 600x600mm
c-c fixed back to roof stucture

built up I-section of 8mm thk m.s.,
finished with two coats of satin white
epoxy paint

built up section of 25mm thk m.s.solid
bar with two 8mm thk m.s. plates fixed
on either side

20x20mm thk aluminum angle as
glazing beading

20mm thk agglomerated white marble
with 3mm thk aluminum strip in-lay

springing point of tree column
structure

built up column (Col. A) made of 8mm
thk m.s. plate

25mm thk specialised exposed
aggregate flooring with 3mm thk
aluminum strip in-lay

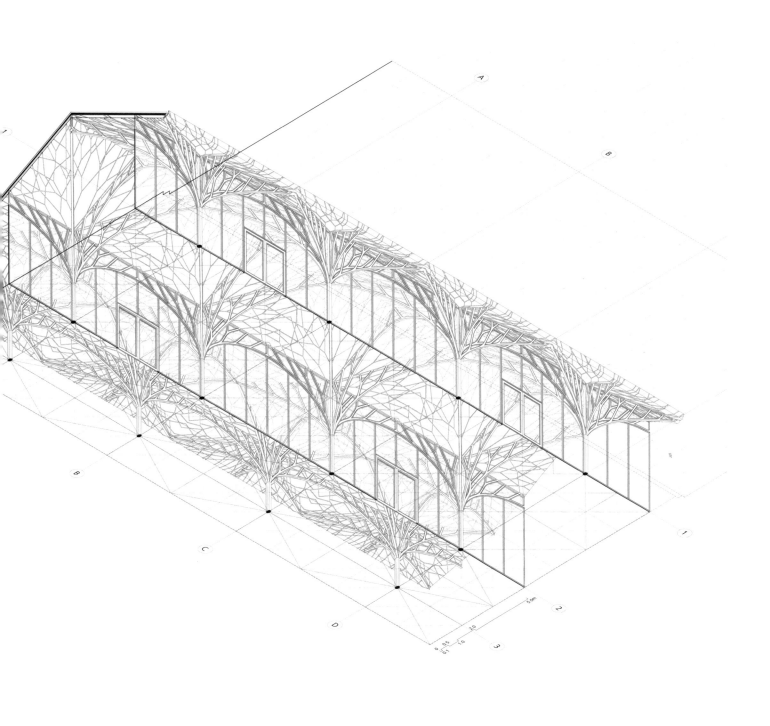

Our proposal attempts to continue this idea of a continuously differentiated space, with no clear boundary, into the envelope of the conservation building.

Matrix of differentiation: branch to vaults

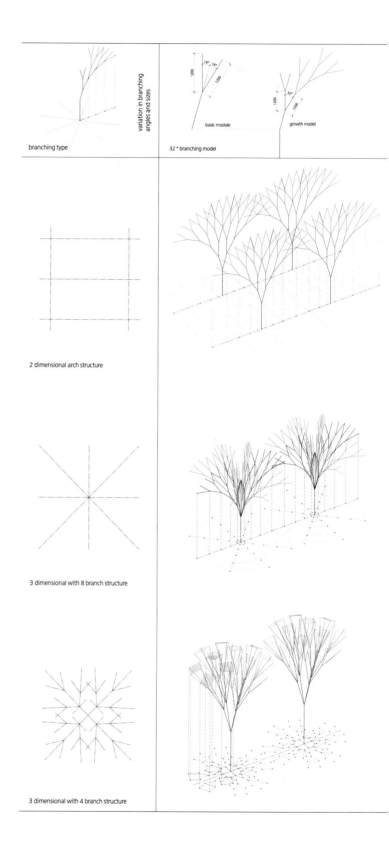

variation in branching angles and sizes

branching type

basic module

growth model

32 ° branching model

2 dimensional arch structure

3 dimensional with 8 branch structure

3 dimensional with 4 branch structure

22

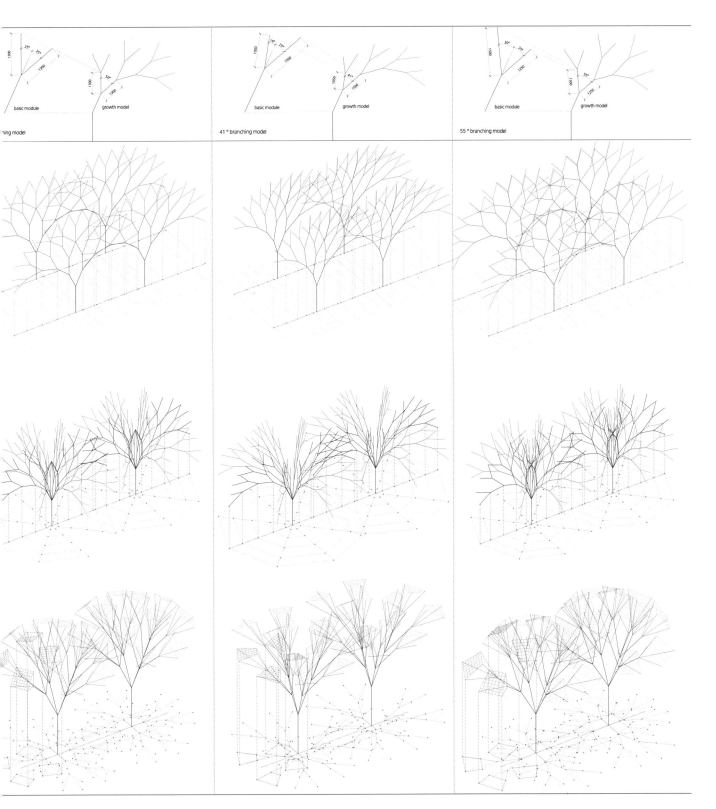

basic module growth model

ning model

41 ° branching model

55 ° branching model

vertical landscaped wall
composed of pvc mesh
planters fixed to a frame of
75x75mm mild steel section

30x60mm mild steel box
canopy,finished with two
coats of matt grey epoxy
paint

38x38mm freestanding
mild steel box
sections,finished with two
coats of matt grey epoxy
paint

25mm thk exposed
aggregate flooring

continuous rainwater
soakaway pit for recharge
of land

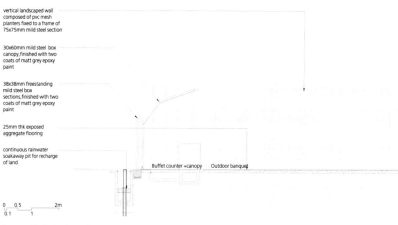

Buffet counter +canopy   Outdoor banquet

0   0.5   2m
0.1   1

Banquet hall short-section

typical T-section of 75 mm ht., 1200mm c/c

typical I-section of 75X75 mm (roof structure)

patterned gypsum board false ceiling, fixed to G.I
framework at 600x600mm c-c

built up I- section of 8 mm thk. mild steel plate,
finished with two coats of satin white epoxy paint

springing point of tree column structure

built-up section of 25 mm thk. m.s. solid bar with
two 8 mm thk. ms plates fixed on either side

20x20 mm thk. alluminium angle as glazing
beading

built-up column (Col. A) made of 8 mm thk. ms
plate

20 mm thk. agglomerated white marble with 3
mm thk. alluminium strip in-lay

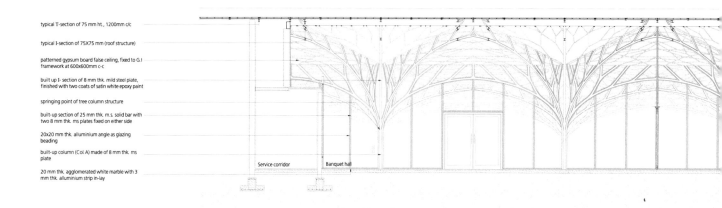

Service corridor   Banquet hall

Banquet hall long-section

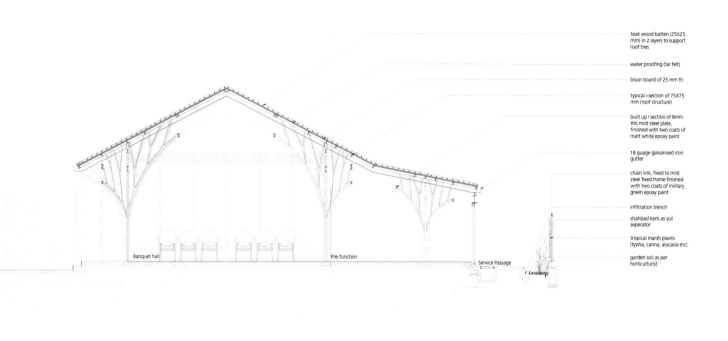

teak wood batten (25X25 mm) in 2 layers to support roof tiles

water proofing (tar felt)

bison board of 25 mm th.

typical i-section of 75X75 mm (roof structure)

built up i section of 8mm thk mild steel plate, finished with two coats of matt white epoxy paint

18 guage galvanised iron gutter

chain link, fixed to mild steel fixed frame finished with two coats of military green epoxy paint

infiltration trench

shahbad kerb as soil seperator

tropical marsh plants (typha, canna, alocasia etc)

garden soil as per horticulturist

Banquet hall

Pre-function

Service Passage

Landscaping

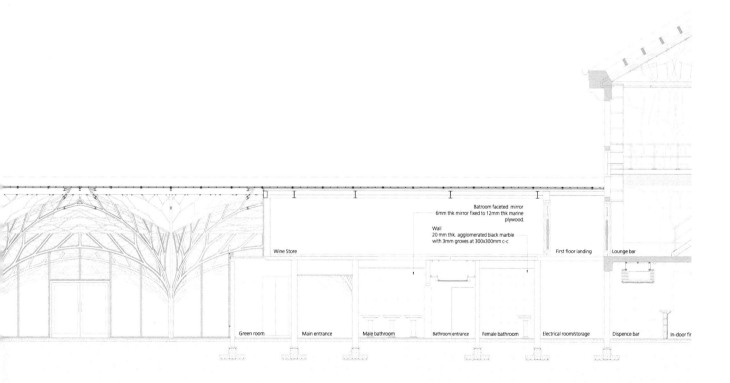

Batroom faceted mirror
6mm thk mirror fixed to 12mm thk marine plywood.

Wall
20 mm thk. agglomerated black marble with 3mm groves at 300x300mm c-c

Wine Store

First floor landing

Lounge bar

Green room

Main entrance

Male bathroom

Bathroom entrance

Female bathroom

Electrical room/storage

Dispence bar

In-door fir

1 Main Entrance
2 Banquet Entrance
3 Service Entrance
4 Open Court
5 Reception
6 Waiting Area
7 Indoor Fine Dine 1
8 Indoor Fine Dine 2
9 Outdoor Fine Dine
10 Pre-Function 1
11 Banquet 1
12 Pre-Function 2
13 Banquet 2
14 Outdoor Banquet
15 Male Washroom
16 Female Washroom
17 Dispense Bar
18 Show Kitchen
19 Bulk Kitchen
20 Service Yard
21 Office
22 Service Passage
23 Store Room
24 Maharaj Kitchen
25 Buffet Counters

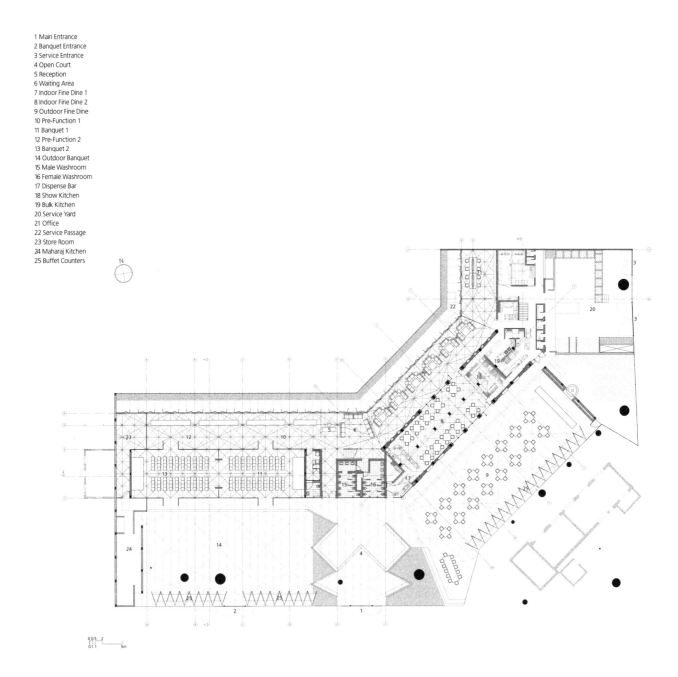

Ground floor plan

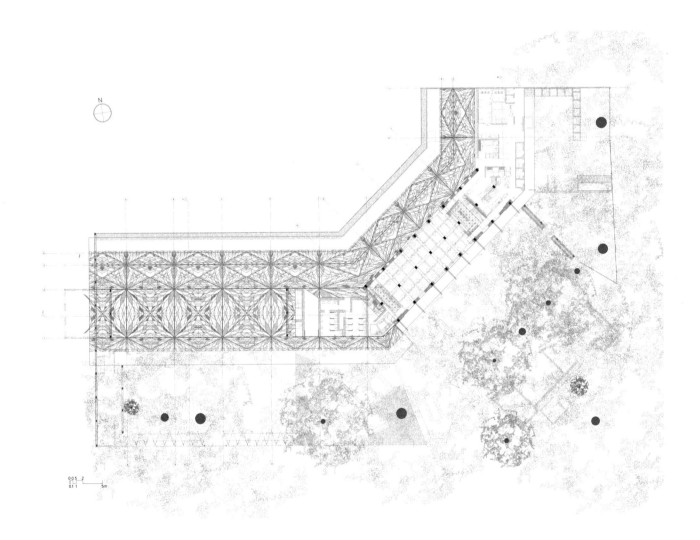

Ground floor reflected ceiling plan

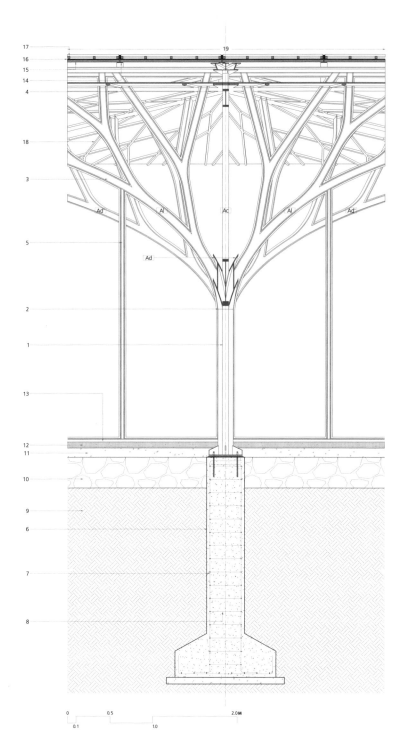

1 built-up column (Col. A) made of 8 mm thk ms plate
2 springing point of tree column structure
3 built up I- section of 8 mm thk mild steel plate,
  finished with two coats of matt white epoxy paint
4 typical I-section of 75 X 75 mm (roof structure)
5 glazing section of built up H- section of 8 mm thk mild steel plate,
  finished with two coats of matt white epoxy paint
6 pedestal of the footing, 450 X 450 mm
7 8 no. T 16
8 T 12 @ 150 mm c/c
9 compact earth
10 rubble masonary
11 p. c. c. slab of required thickness
12 IPS floor to provide uniform surface for terazzo floor
13 specialized terazzo flooring
14 typical T-section of 75 mm ht., 1200mm c/c
15 marine ply of 25 mm th.
16 water proofing (tar felt)
17 teak wood batten (25 X 25 mm) in 2 layers to support roof tiles
18 patterned gypsum board false ceiling
19 roof tiles

Mock-up section detail

34

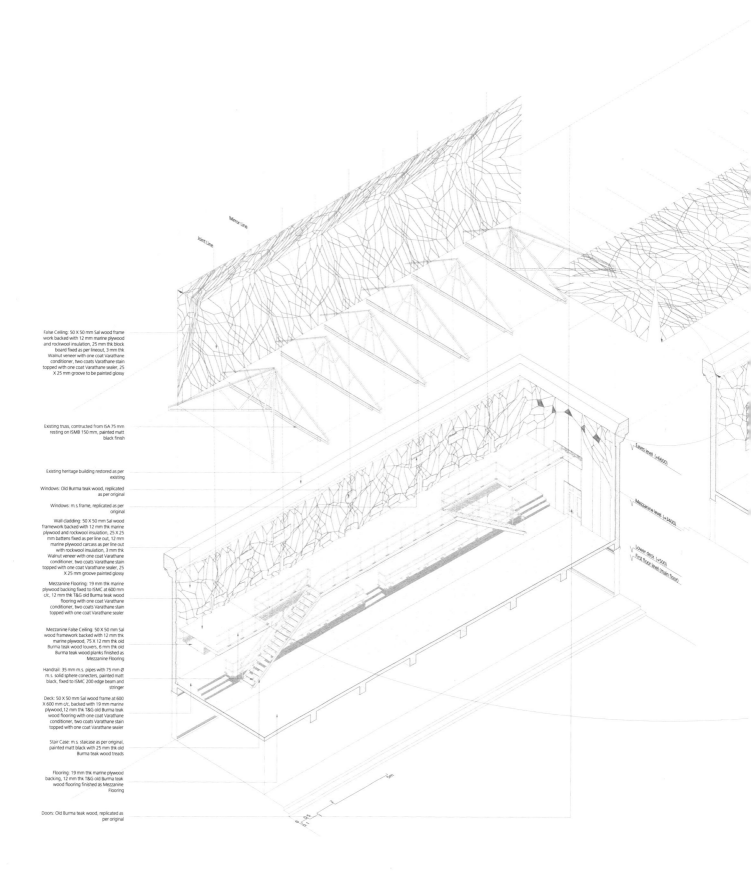

Mirror Line

Joint Line

False Ceiling: 50 X 50 mm Sal wood frame work backed with 12 mm marine plywood and rockwool insulation, 25 mm thk block board fixed as per lineout, 3 mm thk Walnut veneer with one coat Varathane conditioner, two coats Varathane stain topped with one coat Varathane sealer, 25 X 25 mm groove to be painted glossy

Existing truss, contructed from ISA 75 mm resting on ISMB 150 mm, painted matt black finish

Existing heritage building restored as per existing

Windows: Old Burma teak wood, replicated as per original

Windows: m.s. frame, replicated as per original

Wall cladding: 50 X 50 mm Sal wood framework backed with 12 mm thk marine plywood and rockwool insulation, 25 X 25 mm battens fixed as per line out, 12 mm marine plywood carcass as per line out with rockwool insulation, 3 mm thk Walnut veneer with one coat Varathane conditioner, two coats Varathane stain topped with one coat Varathane sealer, 25 X 25 mm groove painted glossy

Mezzanine Flooring: 19 mm thk marine plywood backing fixed to ISMC at 600 mm c/c, 12 mm thk T&G old Burma teak wood flooring with one coat Varathane conditioner, two coats Varathane stain topped with one coat Varathane sealer

Mezzanine False Ceiling: 50 X 50 mm Sal wood framework backed with 12 mm thk marine plywood, 75 X 12 mm thk old Burma teak wood louvers, 6 mm thk old Burma teak wood planks finished as Mezzanine Flooring

Handrail: 35 mm m.s. pipes with 75 mm Ø m.s. solid sphere conecters, painted matt black, fixed to ISMC 200 edge beam and stringer

Deck: 50 X 50 mm Sal wood frame at 600 X 600 mm c/c, backed with 19 mm marine plywood,12 mm thk T&G old Burma teak wood flooring with one coat Varathane conditioner, two coats Varathane stain topped with one coat Varathane sealer

Stair Case: m.s. staicase as per original, painted matt black with 25 mm thk old Burma teak wood treads

Flooring: 19 mm thk marine plywood backing, 12 mm T&G old Burma teak wood flooring finished as Mezzanine Flooring

Doors: Old Burma teak wood, replicated as per original

Eaves level (+6600)

Mezzanine level (+3400)

Lower deck (+500)
First floor level (main floor)

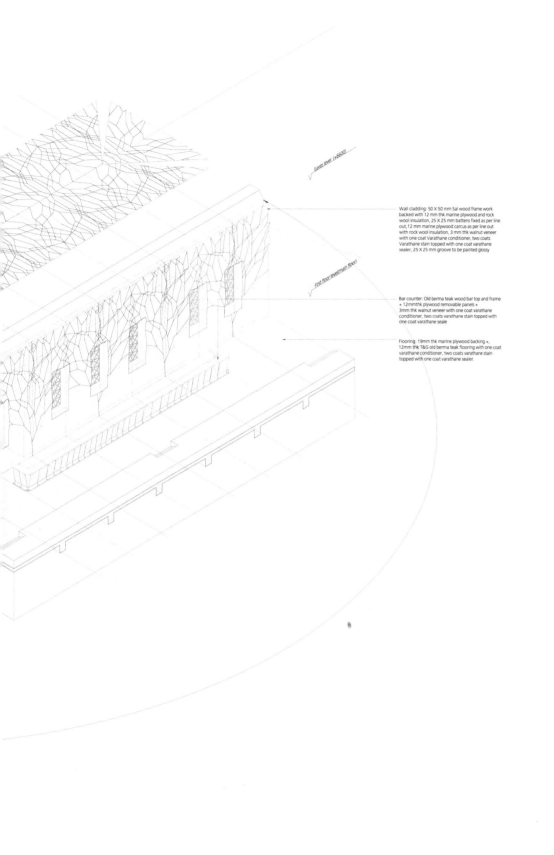

Eaves level (+6600)

First floor level(main floor)

Wall cladding: 50 X 50 mm Sal wood frame work backed with 12 mm thk marine plywood and rock wool insulation, 25 X 25 mm battens fixed as per line out,12 mm marine plywood carcus as per line out with rock wool insulation, 3 mm thk walnut veneer with one coat Varathane conditioner, two coats Varathane stain topped with one coat varathane sealer, 25 X 25 mm groove to be painted glossy

Bar counter: Old berma teak wood bar top and frame + 12mmthk plywood removable panels + 3mm thk walnut veneer with one coat varathane conditioner, two coats varathane stain topped with one coat varathane seale

Flooring: 19mm thk marine plywood backing +, 12mm thk T&G old berma teak flooring with one coat varathane conditioner, two coats varathane stain topped with one coat varathane sealer.

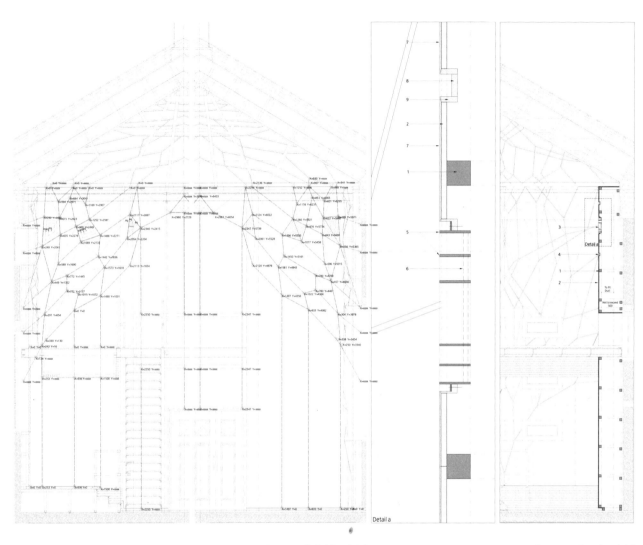

Lounge wall cladding detail   Lounge wall section detail

1   50 X 50 mm Sal wood frame of grid 600 X 600 mm
2   12 mm marine plywood cladding on frame
3   A. C. grill
4   25 X 25 mm 'U' groove
5   3 mm m. s. plate painted black as grill
6   Support for fins
7   3 mm Rosewood veneer with Linseed oil finish
8   12 mm plywood with spray paint finish of approved color
    notched and fixed into Sal wood member
9   3 mm plywood with spray paint finish of approved color

1,3. Completed bar/ lounge space
2. Close-up of wall panel
4,5,6. Construction of the wall panels

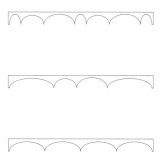

MESWANI HOUSE
2009, PAVNA LAKE, INDIA

The Meswani House is a project that deals with the possibility of utilising a ceiling to capture space and indicate programmatic assignment without resorting to complete vertical enclosures. Located in the beautiful setting of Pavna Lake, our proposal strives to solve two problems often associated with the design of large houses in the countryside – how do you organise ten bedrooms without resorting to long monotonous corridors? And how do you avoid a massing that will be a blot on the beautiful landscape?

Our proposal reconsiders this building type and conceives the organisation of the rooms as an unfolded string of rooms tied together with courtyards and light wells, turning circulation spaces into a series of overlapping semi-outdoor spaces. This encourages the differentiation of the pace of circulation and views along this route and turns the rooms into pavilions strung across the site. The massing of the house is limited to no more than 5m off the ground and the strings of rooms are tiered along the sloping site.

To further tie all the rooms together over a relatively large expanse, a vaulted ceiling is used to accentuate the various rooms and spaces, limiting the use of walls to the most private areas. The vaulted ceiling is created by trimming the various intersecting vaults arranged along the walls of the rotated rooms. These cantilevered vaulted roofs also form the necessary overhangs that shade verandas from the sun and rain. The ceiling plane is further developed on its reversed plane – the roof. In contrast to the ceiling, the roof is left without planar modulations and articulation and remains as flat planes filled with grass, cascading down towards the lake. Thus the ceiling and roof as a clear, legible and singular plane of design gives rise to two autonomous and contiguous spaces for the house – the open landscape planes and the accentuated vaults.

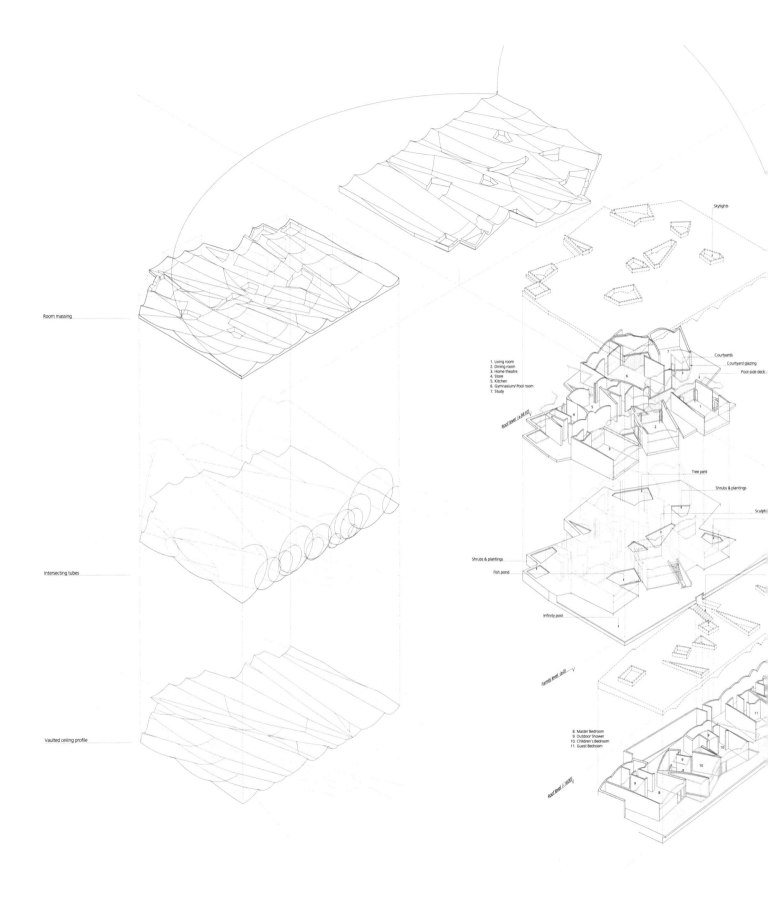

Room massing

Intersecting tubes

Vaulted ceiling profile

Skylights

1. Living room
2. Dining room
3. Home theatre
4. Store
5. Kitchen
6. Gymnasium/ Pool room
7. Study

Courtyards

Courtyard glazing

Pool-side deck

Roof level (+34.10)

Tree yard

Shrubs & plantings

Sculpt()

Shrubs & plantings

Fish pond

Infinity pool

Family level (+0)

8. Master Bedroom
9. Outdoor Shower
10. Children's Bedroom
11. Guest Bedroom

Roof level (-16.00)

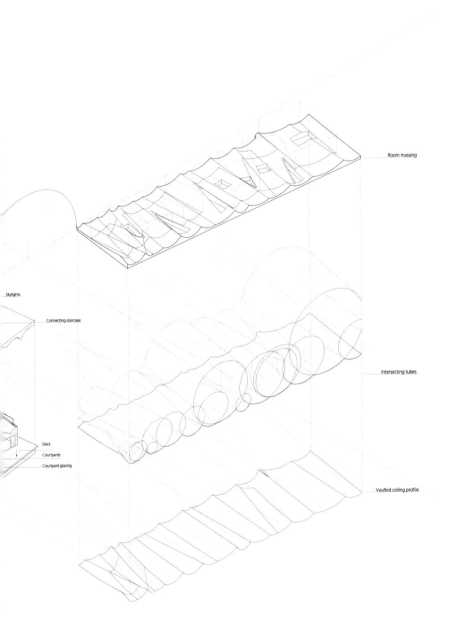

Room massing

Skylights

Connecting staircase

Intersecting tubes

Deck

Courtyards

Courtyard glazing

Vaulted ceiling profile

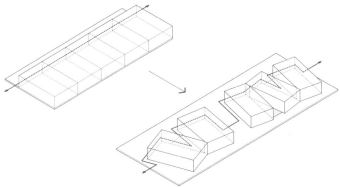

Type change: rooms tied by a long corridor to rooms strung
together by courtyards and lightwells

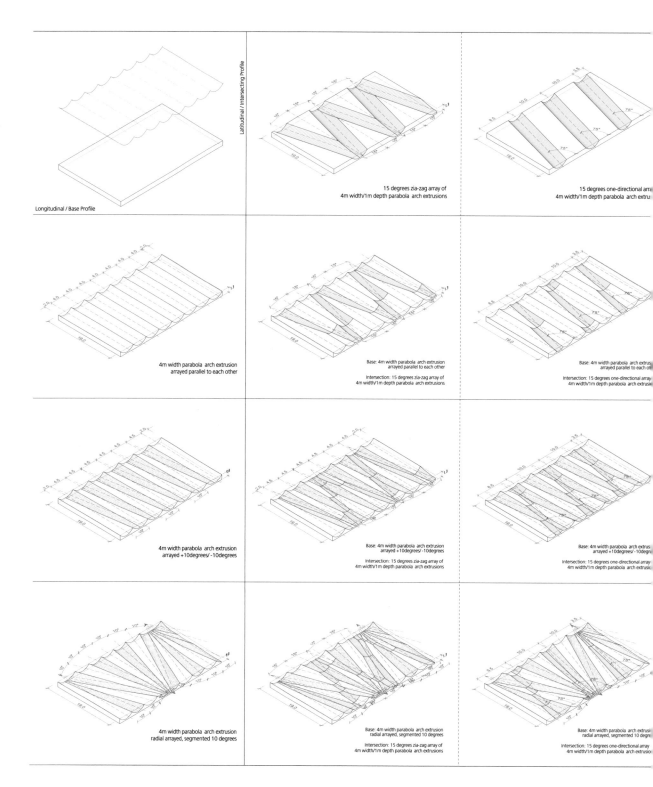

Longitudinal / Base Profile

Latitudinal / Intersecting Profile

15 degrees zia-zag array of
4m width/1m depth parabola arch extrusions

15 degrees one-directional arra
4m width/1m depth parabola arch extru

4m width parabola arch extrusion
arrayed parallel to each other

Base: 4m width parabola arch extrusion
arrayed parallel to each other

Intersection: 15 degrees zia-zag array of
4m width/1m depth parabola arch extrusions

Base: 4m width parabola arch extrusion
arrayed parallel to each o

Intersection: 15 degrees one-directional array
4m width/1m depth parabola arch extrusio

4m width parabola arch extrusion
arrayed +10degrees/ -10degrees

Base: 4m width parabola arch extrusion
arrayed +10degrees/ -10degre

Intersection: 15 degrees zia-zag array of
4m width/1m depth parabola arch extrusions

Base: 4m width parabola arch extrus
arrayed +10degrees/ -10degre

Intersection: 15 degrees one-directional array
4m width/1m depth parabola arch extrusio

4m width parabola arch extrusion
radial arrayed, segmented 10 degrees

Base: 4m width parabola arch extrusion
radial arrayed, segmented 10 degree

Intersection: 15 degrees zia-zag array of
4m width/1m depth parabola arch extrusions

Base: 4m width parabola arch extrus
radial arrayed, segmented 10 degree

Intersection: 15 degrees one-directional array
4m width/1m depth parabola arch extrusio

Matrix of differentiation: tubular intersections to parabolic arches

50

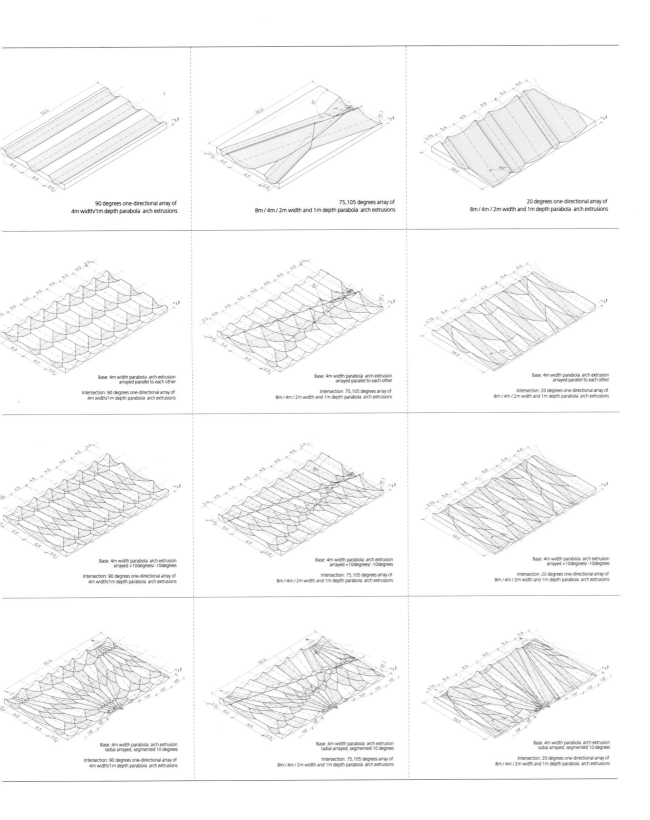

90 degrees one-directional array of
4m width/1m depth parabola arch extrusions

75,105 degrees array of
8m / 4m / 2m width and 1m depth parabola arch extrusions

20 degrees one-directional array of
8m / 4m / 2m width and 1m depth parabola arch extrusions

Base: 4m width parabola arch extrusion
arrayed parallel to each other

Intersection: 90 degrees one-directional array of
4m width/1m depth parabola arch extrusions

Base: 4m width parabola arch extrusion
arrayed parallel to each other

Intersection: 75,105 degrees array of
8m / 4m / 2m width and 1m depth parabola arch extrusions

Base: 4m width parabola arch extrusion
arrayed parallel to each other

Intersection: 20 degrees one-directional array of
8m / 4m / 2m width and 1m depth parabola arch extrusions

Base: 4m width parabola arch extrusion
arrayed +10degrees/-10degrees

Intersection: 90 degrees one-directional array of
4m width/1m depth parabola arch extrusions

Base: 4m width parabola arch extrusion
arrayed +10degrees/-10degrees

Intersection: 75,105 degrees array of
8m / 4m / 2m width and 1m depth parabola arch extrusions

Base: 4m width parabola arch extrusion
arrayed +10degrees/-10degrees

Intersection: 20 degrees one-directional array of
8m / 4m / 2m width and 1m depth parabola arch extrusions

Base: 4m width parabola arch extrusion
radial arrayed, segmented 10 degrees

Intersection: 90 degrees one-directional array of
4m width/1m depth parabola arch extrusions

Base: 4m width parabola arch extrusion
radial arrayed, segmented 10 degrees

Intersection: 75,105 degrees array of
8m / 4m / 2m width and 1m depth parabola arch extrusions

Base: 4m width parabola arch extrusion
radial arrayed, segmented 10 degrees

Intersection: 20 degrees one-directional array of
8m / 4m / 2m width and 1m depth parabola arch extrusions

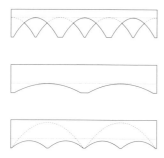

XI'AN 2011 INTERNATIONAL
HORTICULTURAL EXPO MASTERPLAN

2009, XI'AN, CHINA

COMPETITION 2ND PRIZE

Despite our strong desire to win this competition, the opportunity that the site presented led us to rethink the idea of centrality in a city like Xi'an, and compelled us to go beyond the considerations outlined in the design brief – an intellectual adventure, a business risk.

Our proposition addresses two questions: how does the historical city of Xi'an expand beyond its historical centre without dislocating itself into a peripheral condition, and how can the historical elements of the city be relevant in regulating this expansion? The project rethinks the horticultural masterplan, not as a landscape design or architecture that looks like landscape, but as a large architectural artefact, continuing the tradition of city-making in Xi'an.

Although the competition brief called for the design of a greenhouse and associated facilities, our proposal reimagines the role that a horticultural expo can play in seeding and regulating the growth of the city of Xi'an. Our proposal rests on the possibility of using a single architectural artefact to create a new centrality on the periphery of the city, consolidating its peripheral splinters and bridging the existing city and its future growth.

LEARNING FROM XI'AN

It is often assumed that the idea of the city is in opposition to the idea of landscape and nature. More often than not, with landscape architecture projects worldwide today, we are witnessing the endless proliferation of architecture that literally looks like landscape. Our proposal challenges these two tendencies. The history of the city of Xi'an, in particular its city walls, is the starting point for our project. Through this, three strategic ideas are derived as a principle for our proposal. The first attempts to revalidate the tradition of city-making in Xi'an, and to show that elements of the historical city can be relevant and compatible with a horticultural expo park. The second principle rests on the insistence on clarity, where a simple, clear and legible architectural structure can act as a powerful organisational element for an expanded territory many times its scale. The third is contrast, where architecture's pure form and geometry is set in contrast to landscape and nature, without altering the latter. In this way, their contrasting beauty is reinforced.

FIVE CLIMATES CROSSING

We proposed a strong, simple and clear architectural artefact as a main organising element for the masterplan. We began by reconceiving the ubiquitous closed city wall as an unfolded wall, turning it into a linear structure that defines the centre of the site. This one-kilometre linear structure is made up of five greenhouses, each housing a different climate zone. Like the Xi'an city wall this new structure, the Five Climates Crossing, will mark the centre of the park and simultaneously act as a connector, linking the entrance square on the north with Chang'an Park in the middle and the viewing tower on the south. Within the crossing, the greenhouse is arranged linearly as five different episodes of climate zones, allowing visitors to move sequentially from one greenhouse to another whilst maintaining a visual connection to the outside.

IDEA AND MODEL

The typological transformation of the dominant type of the city wall into a linear greenhouse and bridge is governed by both an idea and a model. The idea here can be seen as the strategic reasoning for recentring the site within the context of the city as outlined above. The model, however, points to a set of structural and formal principles that gives rise to a specific organisation. Parabolic vaults are used here to create a differentiated structure that captures varying and rhythmic volumetric conditions and sizes, thus allowing the sequential programming of the structure.

The synthesis of idea and model could also be seen as the utilisation of a disciplinary knowledge (a knowledge of the intrinsic structural, geometric form of the model) to pursue the larger strategic role that architecture can play in the making of the city.

Xi'an city wall

Type change: from a closed city wall to an open wall, from exclusion to incorporation.

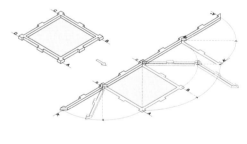

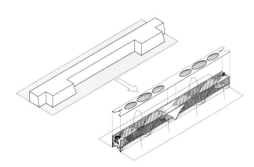

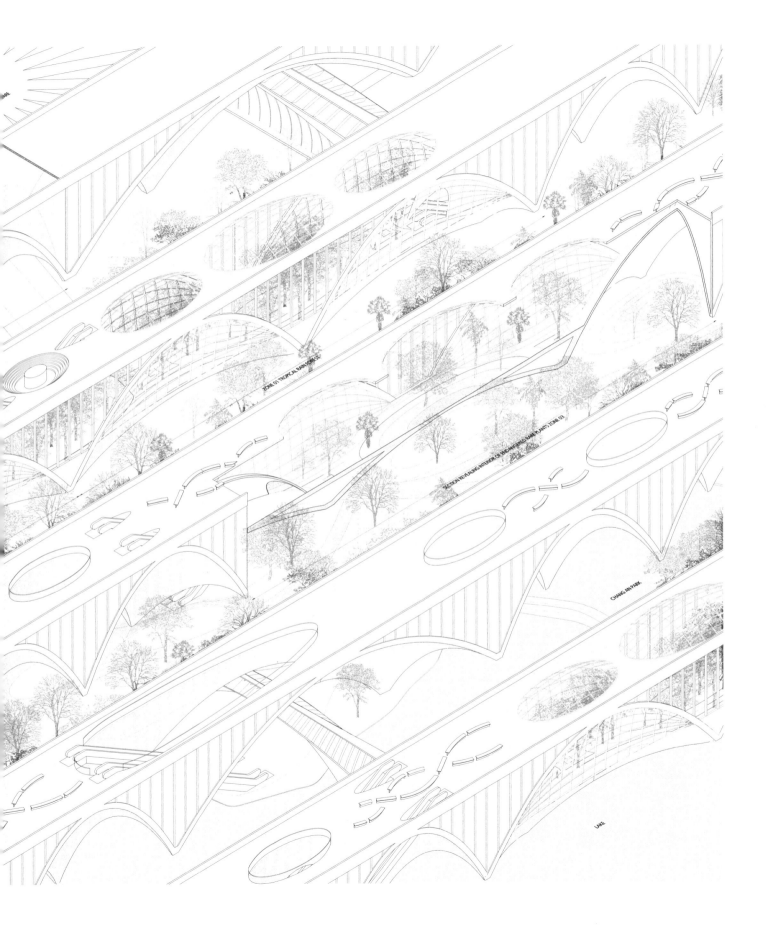

ZONE 01 TROPICAL RAIN FOREST

SECTION REVEALING INTERIOR OF ENDANGERED RARE PLANTS ZONE 03

CHANG AN PARK

LAKE

Matrix of differentiation: parabolic arches to
episodic volumes

Basic bridge Structure

Geometry of the Arches

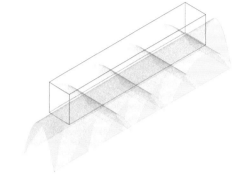

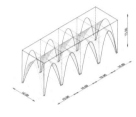

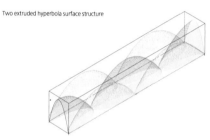

Two extruded hyperbola surface structure

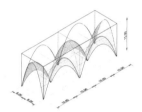

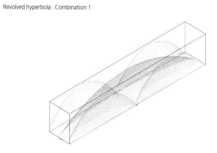

Revolved hyperbola : Combination 1

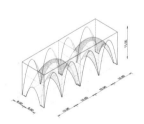

Revolved hyperbola : Combination 2

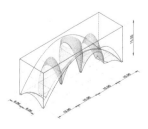

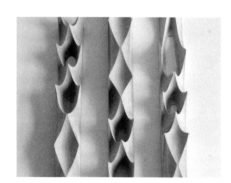

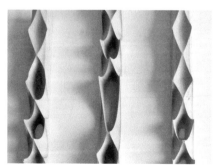

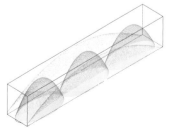

Revolved hyperbola : Combination 3

60

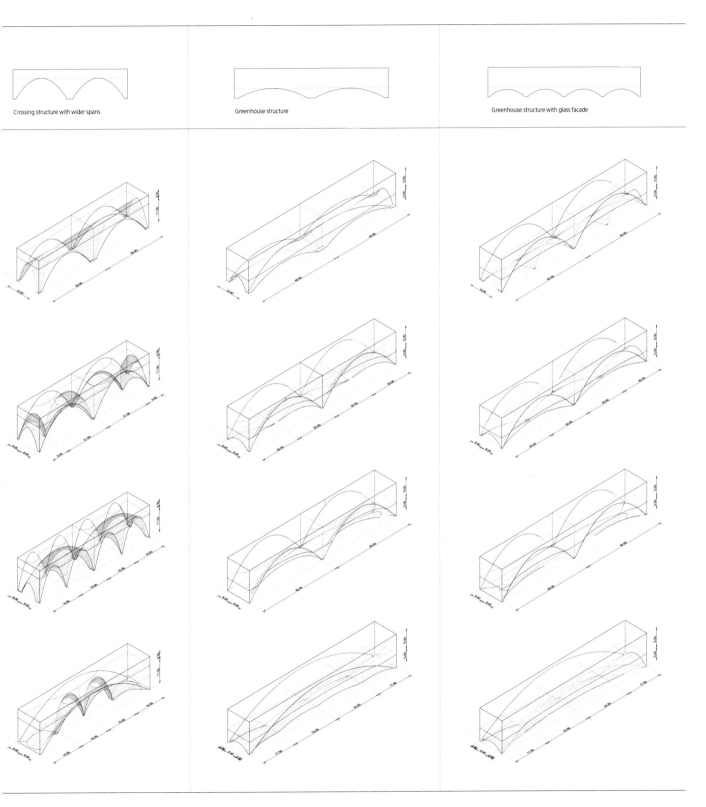

Crossing structure with wider spans

Greenhouse structure

Greenhouse structure with glass facade

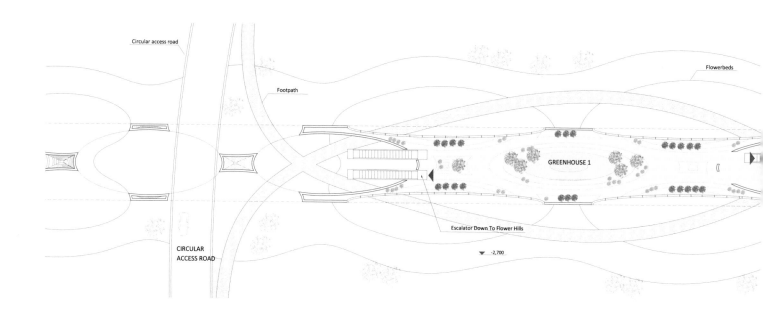

CIRCULAR
ACCESS ROAD

Circular access road

Footpath

Flowerbeds

GREENHOUSE 1

Escalator Down To Flower Hills

▼ -2,700

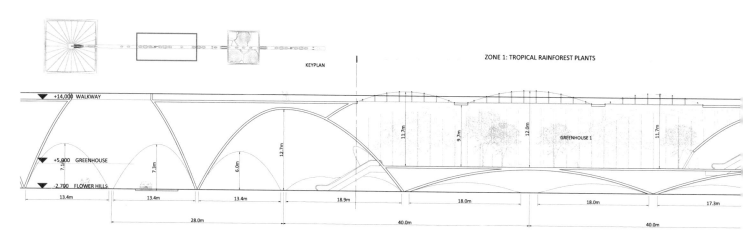

KEYPLAN

ZONE 1: TROPICAL RAINFOREST PLANTS

▼ +14,000 WALKWAY

▼ +5,000 GREENHOUSE

▼ -2,700 FLOWER HILLS

7.1m

12.7m

7.3m

6.0m

11.7m

9.7m

12.0m

GREENHOUSE 1

11.7m

13.4m   13.4m   13.4m   18.9m   18.0m   18.0m   17.3m

28.0m   40.0m   40.0m

0 1 3 5   10   20m

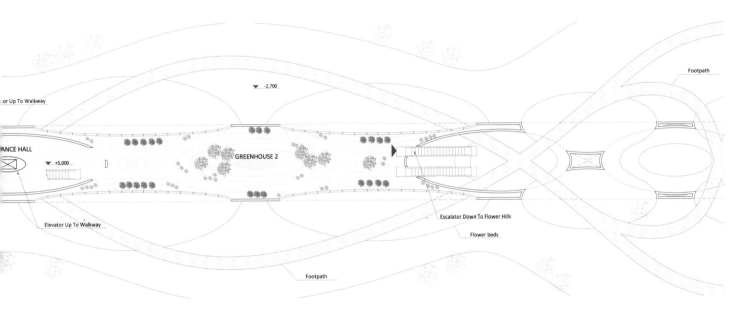

▼ -2,700

Footpath

ANCE HALL

▼ +5,000

GREENHOUSE 2

Elevator Up To Walkway

Escalator Down To Flower Hills

Flower beds

Footpath

Greenhouse plan [+5,000 level]

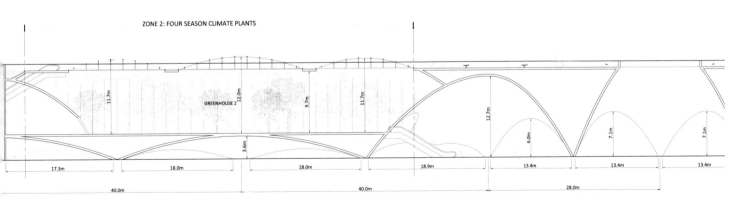

ZONE 2: FOUR SEASON CLIMATE PLANTS

11.7m

GREENHOUSE 2   12.0m

9.7m

11.7m

12.7m

6.0m

7.1m

7.1m

3.6m

17.3m   18.0m   18.0m   18.9m   13.4m   13.4m   13.4m

40.0m   40.0m   28.0m

Greenhouse section

ARCHITECTURE AS MENTAL HABIT

NOTES ON THE METHOD OF SERIE

Pier Vittorio Aureli

In his book *Fundamental Principles of Art History*, Heinrich Wölfflin explained the relevance of reading paintings as part of a series when he said 'each painting depends much more on precedents than on the observation of nature'.[1] According to Wölfflin, the discovery of the structural recurrence of certain common features in different artefacts is what creates the possibility of giving form to an art phenomenon. The making of series is thus the origin of singular works of art.

A similar concept of art was developed by an art historian who, in many other instances, was at the antipodes of Wölfflin's formalist position: Erwin Panofsky. In his short book *Gothic Architecture and Scholasticism*, Panofsky reconstructed a suggestive parallelism between scholastic thought and the gothic architecture that flourished in France between the eleventh and thirteenth centuries.[2] Panofsky speculated that the logical thought that emerged in the development of systematic and intelligible forms of argumentation such as the *disputatio* – the reasoning that proceeds towards its conclusion via a contrapuntal opposition of thesis and antithesis – influenced the development of the gothic as a highly advanced architecture in terms of formal and structural organisation.

Scholasticism as a form of thought emerged as a consequence of the medieval renaissance of cities in Europe. In this context, cultural power shifted from the secluded life of monasteries dispersed in the countryside to the urban life of universities located in the major cities. In the worldly context of cities, the transmission of knowledge solely by means of *lectio* (the meditation on sacred texts typical of the patristical theology of monasteries) was no longer possible. In order to confront the multiplicity of cultural forces typical of a city, theologians developed a form of knowledge based on the dialectical form of *disputatio* in which different points of view such as faith and reason were not assumed to be mutually exclusive, but rather subject to conciliation. In order to sustain such dialectical thought, scholastic theologians developed a method of argumentation in the form of an *a priori* 'grammar of thought' that consisted of a generic scheme of argumentation applicable to any case. This grammar of thought, which

---

1   Heinrich Wölfflin, *Principles of Art History: The Problem of the Development of Style in later art*, trans. M. D. Hottinger (Dover: New York, 1950) 63.
2   Erwin Panofsky, *Gothic Architecture and Scholasticism* (Archabbey Publications: New York 1951).

Panofsky called 'mental habit', was not only a production of knowledge but also the system within which the figures of knowledge were organised in coherent argumentative forms of thought. According to Panofsky, this development in theology had a great influence on the building of cathedrals such as Reims, Amiens, Laon and Chartres. All these artefacts can be considered as a principled whole because their formal and structural aspects belong to the same mental habit. Their form is different, yet their type evolved from the same type of formal and structural solutions that were a fundamental example in Abbé Suger's choir of St Denis. What Panofsky suggested was that the builders of cathedrals, like scholastic theologians, were able to develop such coherent series of forms not by stylistic influence, but because they shared a common grammar from which they could evolve highly specific yet typical forms.

2

The search for a level of coherence that goes beyond iconic recognition – the construction of a mental habit that systematically confronts the complexities and contradictions of the architectural profession – is what characterises the work of Serie. Similar to a *disputatio,* Serie's method is an attempt to negotiate the two extremes of architecture: the commitment to the city and its project, and the definition of an architectural method discernible in its own disciplinary terms. In the last years these two directions of research – urban design and architectural design – have evolved separately. Those committed to urban complexity have elaborated scenarios that are too broad (if not too generic) to become fertile ground for architectural speculation, while those interested in design expertise have retired to the safe ivory tower of digital (parametric) décor.

Serie works towards reconciling the *disputatio* between city and design, and the framework for this reconciliation is the idea of type. According to Serie, the type is in itself a form of conflict between the idea of the project, its 'why do', and the *praxis* of the project, its 'how to'. Serie puts together the two main different ways of thinking about the type: type as the 'idea that must serve as the rule to the model', and type as morphological reasoning on architectural form based on precedents, continuity, repetition and difference. With Serie, this *modus operandi* aims not only for a coherent production but also for a conceptual intelligibility of the method itself, aiming at the production of generic design knowledge. If we look at

projects like the Tote pavilion in Mumbai, the Xi'an International Horticultural Expo and the Bohácky residential masterplan, we realise that the main concern of the designers is not so much the solution to the given brief, but more its use to define architectural elements that may exceed the local context and form a generic architectural grammar. The aim of each design is to extrapolate from the design problem a dominant type whose logic is independent of the problem itself. For example, in the Tote pavilion in Mumbai, the dominant type consists of the invention of a tree-branch structure, a motif that unites structural and aesthetic performance in one spatial form. In the Horticultural Expo the dominant type is the street-in-the-air evolved from the typological form of the ancient city walls. In the Bohácky masterplan the dominant type is the patio-space that operates not only within the house as courtyard, but also around the house in the form of a green wall.

It is possible to describe Serie's architecture as the principled production of types. For this reason their production is best understood through the sequence of projects, rather than in isolation as single design case studies. Serie is less concerned with the originality of each project, than it is with making evident how each project is dependent on a grammar of forms. This may be the reason why the graphic presentation of these projects is so restrained and serial. Like Durand's diagrams, this graphic style suggests that architecture is only understood in the cinematic movement from drawing to drawing, from diagram to diagram, from element to element. In this way the dominant type, like the gothic cathedrals analysed by Panofsky, is identified not as one single case study but as the dynamic transition between cases. Architecture as the production of a mental habit implies operating in the space between projects. This space in between is the mental space of reasoning architecture, not the creation of episodic images ready to be consumed as prêt-à-porter icons, but rather the development of architecture's internal thought.

PUNCTUATED EQUILIBRIUM
THE TYPAL CONVICTION OF SERIE

Sam Jacoby

The work of Serie professes a fundamental concern with 'typological reasoning'. It considers the deep structures of dominant types as part of a diagrammatic series that conflates the idea of the city with that of architecture.[1] The origin of typological reasoning in architecture, and more precisely of the notion of type, was codified in the theories of Quatremère de Quincy, finishing with his seminal entry 'Type' in the *Dictionary of Architecture* of the *Encyclopédie méthodique* in 1825, which was reinterpreted by the neo-rationalists in the 1960s. But seemingly more important to Serie's work is the earlier definition of a typological design method and 'operative theory' by Jean-Nicolas-Louis Durand, whose teaching at the École polytechnique was collected in the *Précis of the Lectures on Architecture* (1802 and 1805). For ideological reasons, architectural historiography has maintained a dichotomous separation between Quatremère's socio-cultural theory of *type* and Durand's formal-functional method of *typology*, asaway of drawing a line between 'classic' modernism and neo-rationalism Serie destabilises this demarcation and explores the potentials of their intersections and overlaps.

The theories of Quatremère and Durand can be contextualised within the eighteenth-century normative discourse of architecture, which demonstrates that by different means they attempted to resolve the same conflict between the authority of the ancients and the emerging need for innovating conventions. Their shared ultimate aim was to establish a new authority and knowledge internal to the discipline of architecture. To further understand the common elements of their approach, one has to revisit Julien-David Le Roy's often overlooked *The Ruins of the Most Beautiful Monuments of Greece* (1758) and especially its second edition of 1770.[2] The crisis of architectural knowledge, stoked by Claude Perrault's view of architecture and beauty as having a conventionalised nature, forced a debate that was represented in the quarrel between the ancients and the moderns. The hallowed principles of architectural orders and proportions were brought into question. Coinciding with an obsession with the

1 For a definition of these terms see Christopher Lee and Sam Jacoby, eds., *Typological Formations: Renewable Building Types and the City* (AA Publications, 2007).

2 In the restructured and enlarged second edition, Le Roy incorporated his writings *History of the Disposition and Different Forms that the Christians Gave to their Temples since the Reign of Constantine the Great to our Own Day* (1764) and *Observations on the Buildings of Ancient Peoples* (1767).

70

question of origins, a new empirical view of history emerged in Le Roy's writings. He was the first to establish in architecture the distinction between history and theory. History, said Le Roy, allowed multiple yet simultaneous origins, expressing the 'primitive original ideas' that can be abstracted, represented and compared in evolutionary typological charts. This view of history informed his theory and provided a synthesis between general metaphysical and more specific materialist readings of a historical architectural object. These preoccupations converged in his typological plates whose representational format and meaning owed much to the scientific taxonomies of Carl Linnaeus' *Systema Naturae* (1735). Tracing the typological development of churches in his *History of the Disposition and Different Forms that the Christians Gave to their Temples since the Reign of Constantine the Great to our Own Day* (1764), Le Roy summarised their evolution in an exceptional taxonomical diagram titled 'Plan of the Most Remarkable Churches Built since the Year 326 until 1764'. In this plate, each stage was related formally and organisationally to its typological predecessor and successor, highlighting its existence as part of a sequence. Its formal reduction and arrangement eliminated the effects of style and (chronological) history; in its place, the comparison visualised an increased tectonic complexification and 'perfection'. Even though Le Roy was not the first to utilise this method (an earlier example was the comparative plate 'Plan of the Churches of St Peter's in Rome and Notre Dame de Paris' by Jacques Tarade of 1713), he recognised its potential as a systematic and descriptive method that could be appropriated in architecture.[3]

Typology's inherent diagrammatic functions hereby supported and disclosed Le Roy's thesis that architectural knowledge could be attained from an abstract historical and formal perspective. At the same, time he believed that the process of perfection could be related back to cultural and social conditions, explaining the developmental differences. In the *Observations on the Buildings of Ancient Peoples* (1767) he wrote, 'in considering some scattered points the line of discoveries that man has made in Architecture [that] we manage to discover its origin, trace its contours and determine its end point', evoking Winckelmann's preface to the *History of the Art of Antiquity* (1764)[4]. In the revised *The Ruins* he posited history as a general ahistorical condition which is contingent and becomes specific within different social, geographical and climatic contexts. Quatremère, whose academic career began with winning the 1785 Prix Caylus, a competition formulated and judged by Le Roy, also owed to Le Roy his interest in multiple origins, the abstract and historicised conditions of architectural evolution, and typological thinking.[5] His theory of type, conceived as forming a social contract between society and architecture, was consistent with Le Roy's understanding of architecture as a sociocultural and geographical phenomenon. Similarly Durand, a former student of Le Roy at the Académie d'architecture, owed to him the analytical and ahistorical potential of typology, which he advanced to an abstract design method, turning its focus from the past towards the present and future. With this Durand implied that architectural composition was in its constitution social and progressive, serving society by fulfilling its needs. This conviction was also expressed in his use of genre rather than type, emphasising his positivist and functionalist doctrine.

Quatremère and Durand agreed on the syntactic function of type, whereby the processes of abstraction acted as the universal grammar transforming the natural preconditions of knowledge into the artificial state of intellection characteristic of an enlightened society. The meaning and possible closure of these artificial languages was guaranteed by socio-cultural and representational conventions of type, which relied on typological specificity and continuity in their principles

3   This plate was published in Tarade's *Desseins de toutes les parties de l'église de Saint Pierre de Rome* (1713). Following this, a number of similar plates by Juste-Aurèle Meissonnier in *Parallèle général des edifices les plus considérables depuis les Egyptiens, les Grecs jusqu'à nos derniers modernes* (c. 1757) and Gabriel-Pierre-Martin Dumont in *Parallèle de monuments sur une meme échelle* in *Détail des plus intéressantes parties d'architecture de la basilique Saint-Pierre de Rome* (1763) appeared. These examples were likely to be known by Le Roy, see Robin Middleton's introduction to Le Roy's *The Ruins of the Most Beautiful Monuments of Greece*, trans. David Britt (Getty Research Institute, 2004) 90–97.

4   Le Roy, 'Réflexions préliminaires' in *Observations sur les édifices des anciens peuples*, trans. Jeanne Kisacky in 'History and Science: Julien-David Leroy's "Dualistic Method of Architectural History"' in *Journal of the Society of Architectural Historians*, 60: 3 (2001) 260–89.

5   The Prix Caylus essay by Quatremère was titled after the question raised by Le Roy: *Mémoire sur cette question: Quel fut l'Etat de l'architecture chez les Égyptiens, et qu'est-ce que les Grecs en ont emprunté?* (Mémoire on the Question: What was the state of Egyptian architecture and what have the Greeks borrowed from it?). For Le Roy's involvement in the competition see, Sylvia Lavin, *Quatremère de Quincy and the Invention of a Modern Language of Architecture* (MIT Press, 1992).

and rules. Quatremère famously distinguished between type (as owing to a metaphysical neoplatonic idea, delivering a true imitation in abstraction) and model, as a minor imitation or copy of nature through precedents. Quatremère and Durand were further unified in their concern with a redefinition of the 'ideal' destination of architecture through its 'classical' functions: representation, reason, and history, or meaning, truth, and continuity.[6] The resultant tension between 'generic knowledge' and 'specific architectural response', between cultural heritage and formal precedent, between political agency and functional utility is also evident in the work of Serie. Pursuing a typological reasoning that incorporates the potentials of type and typology, Serie confidently returns to the subject of history and reason through the continuity, analysis and interpretation afforded by typology. Despite a deceptive proximity to Durand's aesthetic, however, Durand's essential problem of meaning, in the sense of representation, is absent in Serie or perhaps simply no longer experienced as contentious. In place of a compositional method and procedural coherence, we find certain traces of inevitable authorial aesthetics and choices, but more significantly a willingness to engage with a different kind of coherence that relies on ideas and in particular the idea from and for the city.

The projects by Serie are developed from a typological conflict that instigates a conversation between project-specific parameters and the generic deep structures of 'Vaults', 'Circles' and 'Grids', which are used to group the different investigations. From these essentially scale-less formal organisations are derived the later multi-scalar tectonic differentiations that give each scheme its specificity and logic. Consequently, it is noticeable that under the taxonomy of 'Ceiling/Vaults', the vault is utilised less for its obvious structural behaviour and more as an organisational device for restructuring The Tote, Meswani House and Xi'an Masterplan into the smaller spatial, volumetric and programmatic units required by the brief. The same organisational function can be detected in the Blue Frog, Factory H, Huaxi Urban Centre, and Boháčky Masterplan, taxonomised under 'Plan/Circles' or the 'Facade/Grids' projects of V Office and Ružinov Housing.

6   This definition of the 'classical' owes to Peter Eisenman, 'The End of the Classical: The End of the Beginning, the End of the End' in *Perspecta* 21 (1984) 155–73.

If we are to understand the projects as belonging to a series under the same taxonomical heading, there has to be a rational consistency that relates them. The given deep structure, however, does not quite provide us with the required criteria. Unlike other recent and familiar architectural taxonomies employed by UNStudio as design models or FOA in phylum – which are premised on a prototypical cataloguing and retrieval of generic morphological 'species' that adapt to the particular requirements of a project – Serie starts from an explicit typological condition: thus from a specific architectural problem. The 'idea' and 'conflict' that emerge from this problem are however neither morphologically or programmatically precise nor procedurally and sequentially explicable (as was the case with Durand, for example). Instead, by considering typological precedent, an attempt is made to define a type change which subverts the received form into a new potential organising principle and diagram, allowing disparate typological strategies within the same taxonomic grouping. To use an evolutionist term, this 'punctuated equilibrium', denoting 'very rapid events of speciation', causes a recognisable transformation of the precedent organisation into a new configuration. [7] For example, with the Blue Frog we find a type change that hybridises a horseshoe theatre with a restaurant layout (typological precedent). In the case of the Bohácky masterplan, there is an inversion of the Cartesian city grid (morphological precedent), resulting in its functional and typological reversal. In this sense, the classification by formal traits distracts from the fact that their coherence primarily derives from the attempt to define a conceptual (rather than technique- or procedure-dependent) typological rupture, one that is consequently not predicated on formal, morphological or programmatic but on strategic and intellectual similarity. Only then are the deep structures employed to provide the tactical means to articulate a project and ensure a level of organisational consistency.

The established conceptual coherence underlying the classification is further complicated by the fact that type refers to typology, which in turn refers to the city. The relationship between architecture and the city, undeniably a central theme in Aldo Rossi, but already inevitable since the fusion of prototypes and town planning in the modern movement, is employed by Serie not as a historical or anti-historical condi-tion, but as an idea from and for the city. This means that history and architecture can be selectively decontextualised before being speculatively and projectively reconstructed as an architectural idea and diagram – or as a catalyst punctuating the equilibrium – that embodies critical conditions of the city. The city is understood through abstracted dominant types and affected by means of typological and architectural production. The coexistence between history (generic precedents and evolution) and architecture (specific material articulation and context), as anticipated by Le Roy and developed into typological theories at the turn of the nineteenth century, is critically revisited and creates in the work of Serie the possibility of a new typological reasoning that reclaims for the practice of architecture an intelligent influence on, and a new knowledge of, the formation of the city.

7   See Stephen Jay Gould and Niles Eldredge, 'Punctuated Equilibria: The Tempo and Mode of Evolution Reconsidered' (*Paleobiology* 3, 1977) 115–51.

DEEP STRUCTURE 2

PLAN / CIRCLES

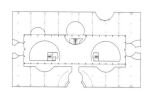

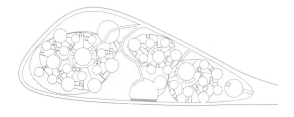

Blue Frog Acoustic Lounge, Mumbai   Xin Tian Di Factory H, Hangzhou   Parcel 9, HX Urban Centre, Guizhou

Bohácky Residential Masterplan, Bratislava

BLUE FROG ACOUSTIC LOUNGE
2006-07, MUMBAI, INDIA

The strategies of hybridisation of the 90s, more often than not, resulted in the smooth blending of one tectonic surface with another. Accompanying this tendency was the belief that the formal procedure of blending would naturally result in the cross-breeding of programme.

Blue Frog for us is a project that revisits the problem of multi-programmed spaces without resorting to formal redundancy as a representation of programmatic complexity.

The project brief called for the conversion of a large north-lit industrial warehouse in Mumbai's old mill district into sound recording studios and an acoustic lounge. The lounge consists of a restaurant, bar and a live stage. Beyond this amalgamation of provisions, Blue Frog seeks to stage an acoustic experience *par excellence*.

Based on this desire of the project brief to have it all, the question for us was: how do you collapse a theatre, restaurant, bar and club into a warehouse whilst maintaining all the performative characteristics of each individual type?

The deep structure that has been employed is of a cellular organisation composed of circles of varying sizes approximating a horse-shoe configuration in plan. The differential extrusions of these circles, encapsulated at different levels as tiered cylindrical seating booths, allow the sight lines of diners and standing patrons to be distributed across staggered levels that increase in height away from the stage. The booths seat four to ten people and are arranged around an open centre that can either double up as a potential 360 degree stage or accommodate standing patrons, bringing them closer to the main stage to create an intimate viewing experience. The mahogany-panelled cylindrical booths not only maintain uninterrupted views of the stage, but also establish a constant distance between diners, irrespective of how crowded the lounge gets.

The undulating height of the seating booths is gently modulated by a glowing acrylic resin surface which unifies the disparate types and retains the presence of the architecture even in the midst of the spectacle of a sound and light show.

It can be argued that the programmatic multiplicities here arise out of the disposition of the irreducible typal imprints harnessed from the above-mentioned precedent types. And it is these deep structures which give rise to the multiple programmatic configurations without resorting to any strategies of formal convolution.

Based on the desire of the project brief to have it all, the question for us was how do you collapse a theatre, restaurant, bar and club into a warehouse whilst maintaining all the performative characteristics of each individual type?

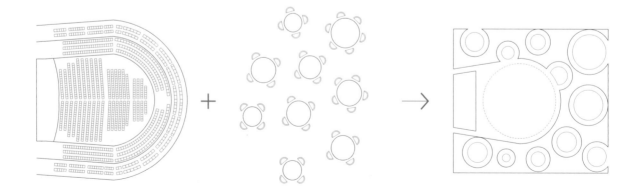

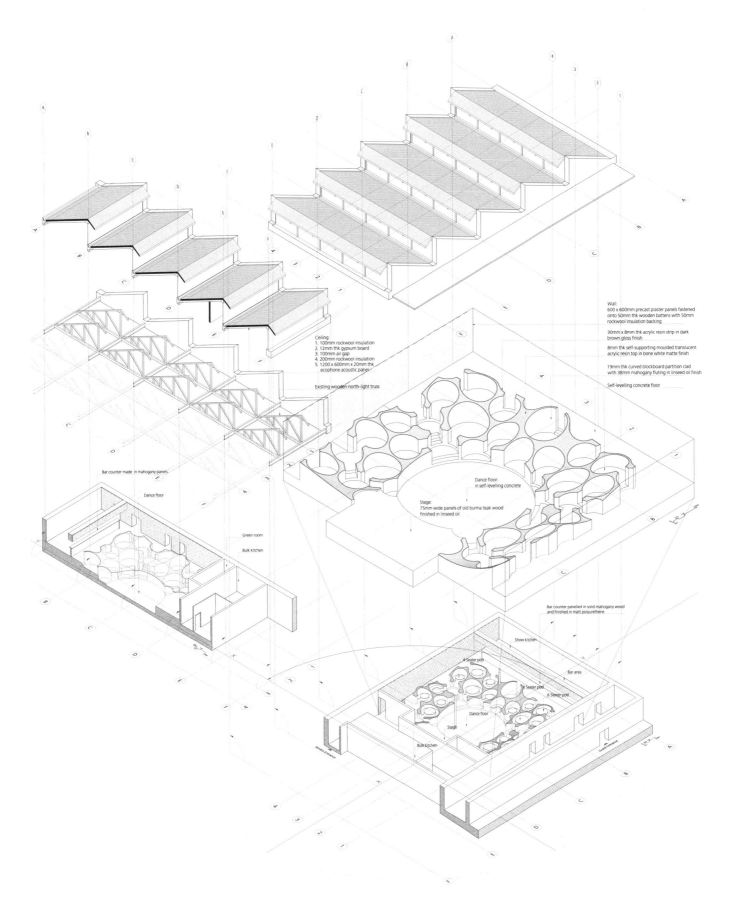

Ceiling:
1. 100mm rockwool insulation
2. 12mm thk gypsum board
3. 100mm air gap
4. 200mm rockwool insulation
5. 1200 x 600mm x 20mm thk ecophone acoustic panel

Existing wooden north-light truss

Wall:
600 x 600mm precast plaster panels fastened onto 50mm thk wooden battens with 50mm rockwool insulation backing

30mm x 8mm thk acrylic resin strip in dark brown gloss finish

8mm thk self-supporting moulded translucent acrylic resin top in bone white matte finish

19mm thk curved blockboard partition clad with 38mm mahogany fluting in linseed oil finish

Self-levelling concrete floor

Bar counter made in mahogany panels

Dance floor

Green room

Bulk kitchen

Dance floor:
in self-levelling concrete

Stage:
75mm wide panels of old burma teak wood finished in linseed oil

Bar counter panelled in solid mahogany wood and finished in matt polyurethene

Show kitchen

4 Seater pod

Bar area

8 Seater pod

6 Seater pod

Dance floor

Stage

Bulk kitchen

Matrix of differentiation:
aggregation of circles towards a horse-shoe plan

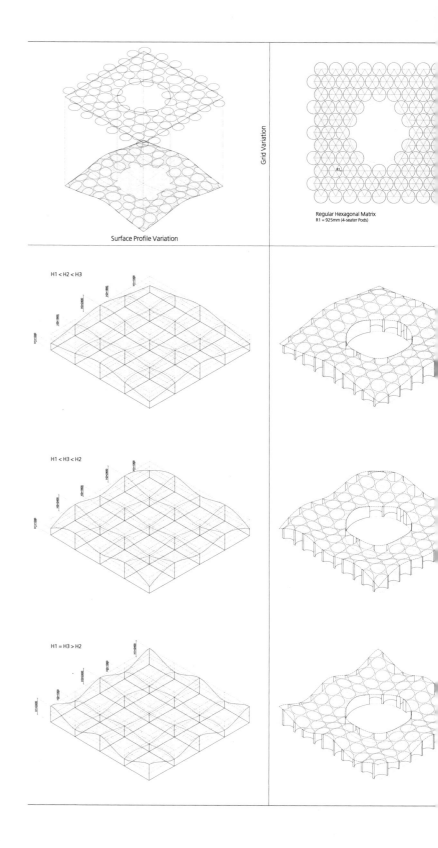

Grid Variation

Surface Profile Variation

Regular Hexagonal Matrix
R1 = 925mm (4-seater Pods)

H1 < H2 < H3

H1 < H3 < H2

H1 = H3 > H2

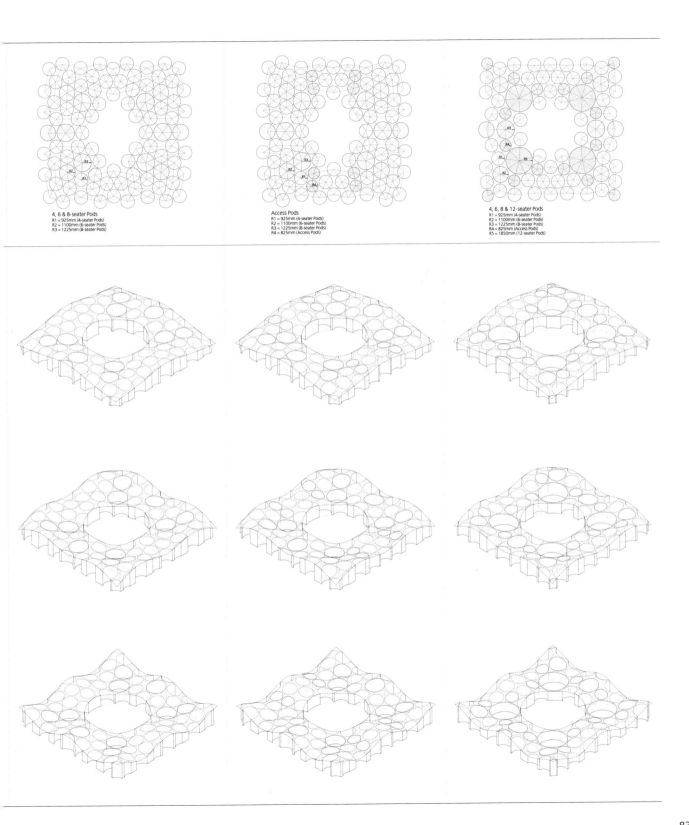

4, 6 & 8-seater Pods
R1 = 925mm (4-seater Pods)
R2 = 1100mm (6-seater Pods)
R3 = 1225mm (8-seater Pods)

Access Pods
R1 = 925mm (4-seater Pods)
R2 = 1100mm (6-seater Pods)
R3 = 1225mm (8-seater Pods)
R4 = 825mm (Access Pods)

4, 6, 8 & 12-seater Pods
R1 = 925mm (4-seater Pods)
R2 = 1100mm (6-seater Pods)
R3 = 1225mm (8-seater Pods)
R4 = 825mm (Access Pods)
R5 = 1850mm (12-seater Pods)

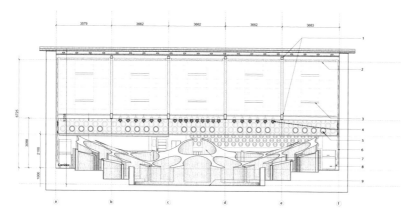

Section across the dance floor

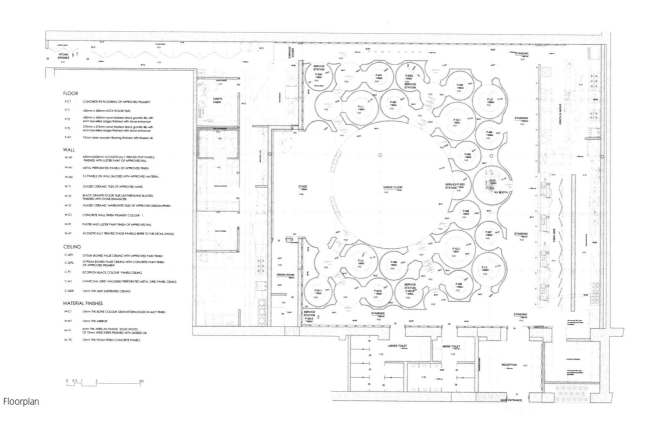

FLOOR

F-C1   CONCRETE IPS FLOORING OF APPROVED PIGMENT.

F-T1   450mm x 585mm KOTA FLOOR TILES

F-T2   450mm x 450mm sand blasted black granite tile with
       6mm bevelled edges finished with stone enhancer

F-T3   375mm x 375mm sand blasted black granite tile with
       6mm bevelled edges finished with stone enhancer

F-W1   75mm wide wooden flooring finished with linseed oil.

WALL

W-AP   600mmx600mm ACOUSTICALLY TREATED POP PANELS,
       FINISHED WITH LUSTER PAINT OF APPROVED RAL.

W-M1   METAL PERFORATED PANELS OF APPROVED FINISH.

W-M2   S.S PANELS ON WALL BACKED WITH APPROVED MATERIAL.

W-T1   GLAZED CERAMIC TILES OF APPROVED MAKE.

W-T2   BLACK GRANITE FLOOR TILES LEATHER/SAND BLASTED,
       FINISHED WITH STONE ENHANCER.

W-T3   GLAZED CERAMIC MARBONITE TILES OF APPROVED DESIGN/FINISH.

W-C1   CONCRETE WALL FINISH PIGMENT COLOUR - 1

W-P1   PASTER AND LUSTER PAINT FINISH OF APPROVED RAL

W-AT   ACOUSTICALLY TREATED STAGE PANELS(REFER TO THE DETAIL DWGS)

CEILING

C-GP1   GYPSUM BOARD FALSE CEILING WITH APPROVED PAINT FINISH

C-GP2   GYPSUM BOARD FALSE CEILING WITH CONCRETE PAINT FINISH
        OF APPROVED PIGMENT

C-P1   ECOPHON BLACK COLOUR PANELS CEILING

C-M1   CHARCOAL GREY ANODISED PERFORATED METAL GRID PANEL CEILING

C-MDF   12mm THK MDF SUSPENDED CEILING

MATERIAL FINISHES

M-C1   10mm THK BONE COLOUR GRANAFORM/SOLEX IN MATT FINISH

M-M1   12mm THK MIRROR

M-V1   6mm THK AFRICAN PADOK SOLID WOOD,
       OF 75mm WIDE STRIPS WITH LINSEED OIL.

M-FC   12mm THK FOAM FINISH CONCRETE PANELS

0 0.5 1   2   5m

Floorplan

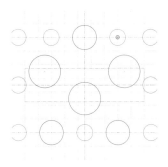

XIN TIAN DI FACTORY H
2010-ONGOING, HANGZHOU, CHINA

Construction to begin in January 2011

In March 2010 Serie, alongside Grimshaw of London and Pysall Ruge Arkitekten of Berlin, were selected to renovate and design four large disused factories in Hangzhou, with Serie and Pysall Ruge each designing one of the four factories, and Grimshaw the remaining two. These factories will form the main urban core for a new urban core, named Hangzhou Xin Tian Di, located 6km northeast of the present city centre.

It became apparent early on that the project faced several conflicting demands. For the project to be economically viable, an insertion of floor areas totalling four times its original footprint would have to be accommodated. On the other hand, filling up the factory would completely diminish its most unique feature – its 16m-high volume. Thus our main concern is to preserve the main hall of the factory as a spectacular internal volume and to accentuate the industrial drama of this massive void by restoring the concrete truss roof structure and by bringing additional light down through a newly glazed lantern. In addition, we are preserving and restoring the other important elements of the original factory design: the crumbling brick facade, the rusting mobile crane, the brick-built industrial chimney and the grand concrete colonnade.

To abstain from the architectural crime of filling the entire main hall with programme, we placed the supporting facilities – shops, restaurants, bars and creative offices – in a surrounding plinth This plinth acts as a device to emphasise the main factory building: in one sense it frames the factory, in another it serves as a pedestal above that brings us face to face with the factory. As well as absorbing programme and supporting the factory, the top surface of the plinth gently undulates and is punctured with green patios and water bodies, constituting an abstraction and re-reading of the natural landscape of Hangzhou.

The utilisation of the same deep structure as Blue Frog (Plan/Circles) for this project enabled us to rethink the idea of the mat building as a plinth. Here the plinth serves to punctuate the factory as the anchor for the masterplan, with surrounding buildings many times its density. This alternative strategy eschews the reliance on hyper-dense buildings that accumulate pedestrian flows. Instead, it presents the reclaimed void as a new urban core.

XinTianDi Masterplan, Hangzhou, China

Existing factory: facade, concrete crane structure and chimney

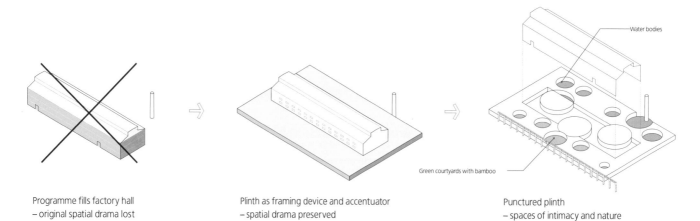

Programme fills factory hall
– original spatial drama lost

Plinth as framing device and accentuator
– spatial drama preserved

Punctured plinth
– spaces of intimacy and nature

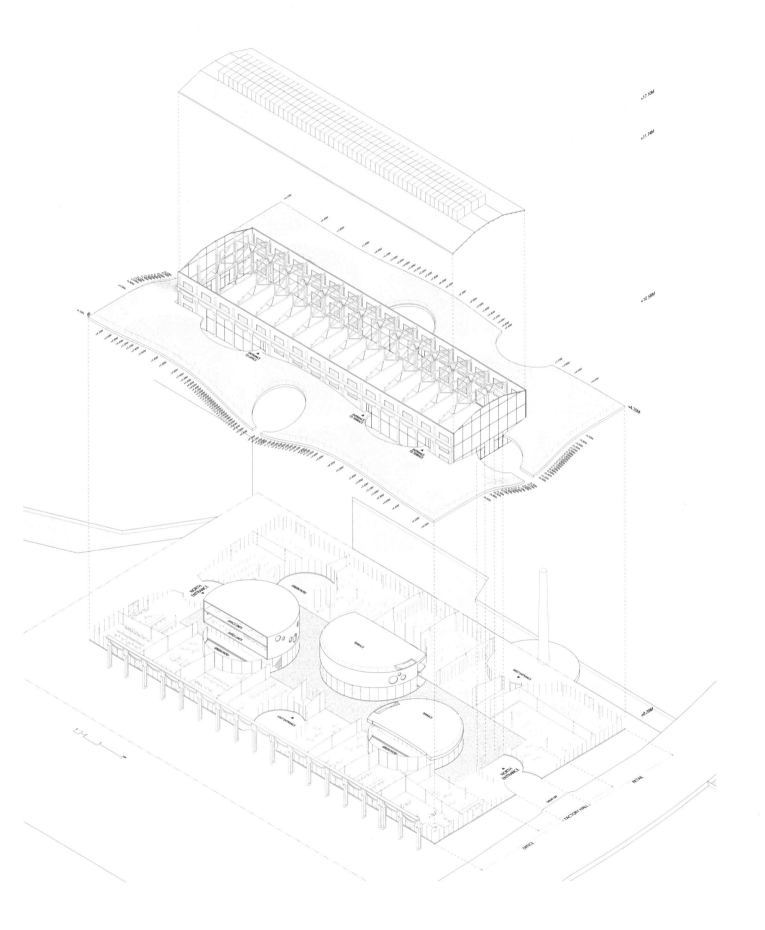

1 Factory hall
2 Concrete truss
3 Brickwork of the facade

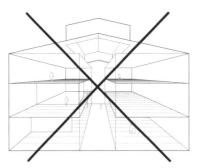
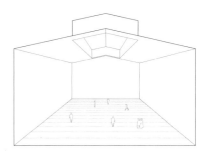

This factory area is the most important. It is this dramatic open space that will be the key to the success of the project. Freeing the space from programme is the most fundamental element of our conservation strategy.

Matrix of differentiation:
aggregation of circles and
solid/void reversals

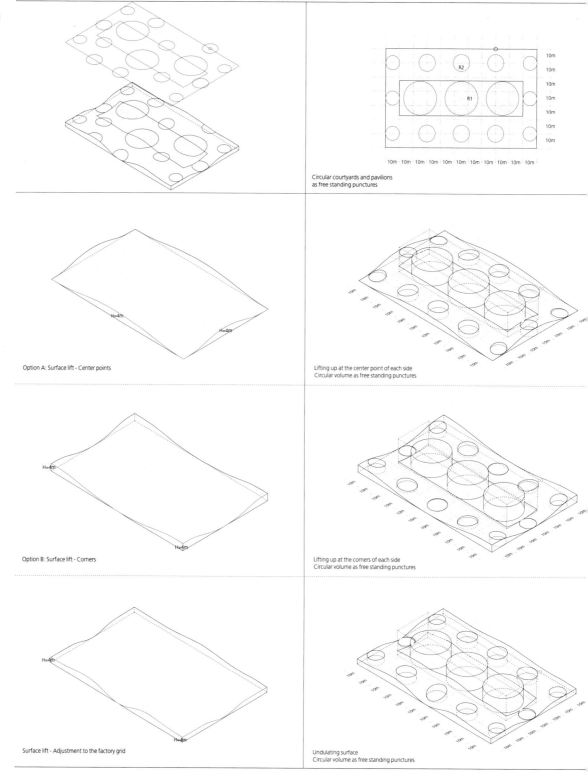

Circular courtyards and pavilions
as free standing punctures

Option A: Surface lift - Center points

Lifting up at the center point of each side
Circular volume as free standing punctures

Option B: Surface lift - Corners

Lifting up at the corners of each side
Circular volume as free standing punctures

Surface lift - Adjustment to the factory grid

Undulating surface
Circular volume as free standing punctures

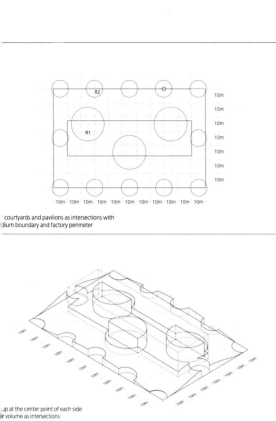

courtyards and pavilions as intersections with
dium boundary and factory perimeter

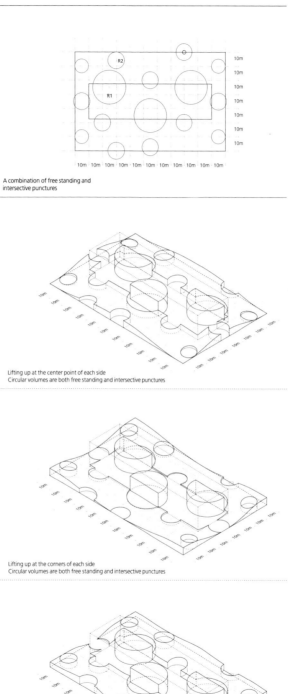

A combination of free standing and
intersective punctures

up at the center point of each side
r volume as intersections

Lifting up at the center point of each side
Circular volumes are both free standing and intersective punctures

up at the corners of each side
r volume as intersections

Lifting up at the corners of each side
Circular volumes are both free standing and intersective punctures

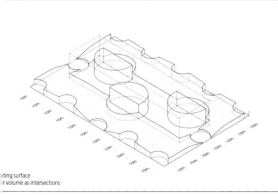

ting surface
r volume as intersections

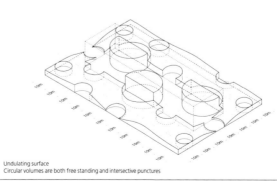

Undulating surface
Circular volumes are both free standing and intersective punctures

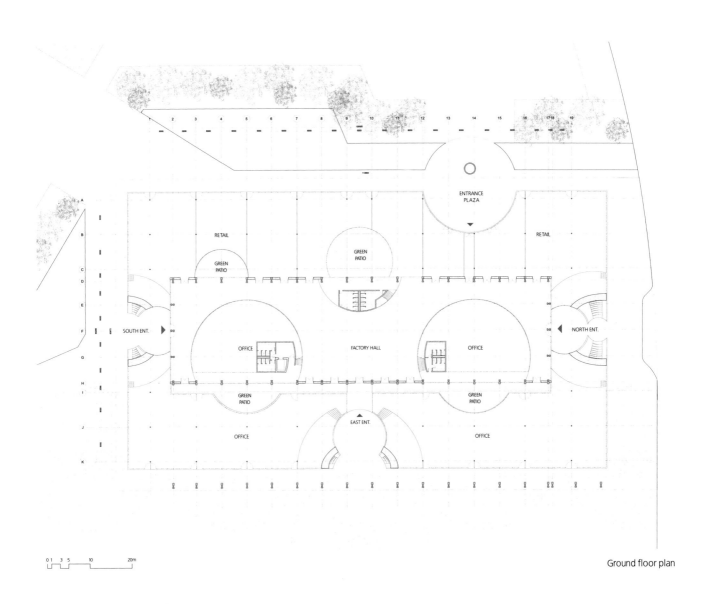

GREEN
PATIO

RETAIL

ENTRANCE
PLAZA

RETAIL

GREEN
PATIO

SOUTH ENT.

OFFICE

FACTORY HALL

OFFICE

NORTH ENT.

GREEN
PATIO

GREEN
PATIO

OFFICE

EAST ENT.

OFFICE

0 1 3 5   10   20m

Ground floor plan

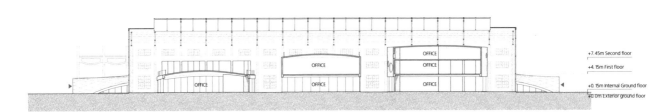

+7.45m Second floor

+4. 15m First floor

OFFICE

OFFICE

OFFICE

OFFICE

OFFICE

OFFICE

+0.15m Internal Ground floor

+0.0m Exterior ground floor

Section

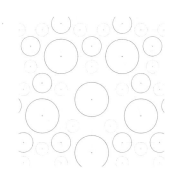

PARCEL 9, HX URBAN CENTRE
2008, GUIZHOU, CHINA

In 2008 Serie was invited along with nine other young architectural practices from across the globe to participate in the design of a new urban centre in Guizhou. The masterplan, developed by MAD Beijing and Tongji Studio 6, envisioned autonomous buildings surrounded by nature – in retrospect, perhaps the only strategy able to accommodate the different architects in the absence of stringent design guidelines.

Our allocated site, Parcel 9, is the first parcel in the south cluster of low-rise buildings, set in contrast to the tower cluster on the north, as intended by the masterplanners. Our proposal attempted to rethink the courtyard house in the context of high-density communal housing and to reconsider the synthesis of a legible figure with the surrounding landscape. From this, it draws together two ideas, one typological, the other from the indigenous landscape of Guizhou. The project begins with the typal transformation of the Hakka/Tulou house, with its circular courtyards, proposing a collectively shared circular courtyard that binds together a series of smaller private courtyards – the focal point for the proposed SOHOs (Single Occupier Home Offices), a new live/work type. With its clustering of courtyards, the communal housing is conceived as an amalgamation of different degrees of private and shared spaces cohering into a legible whole. The placement of the multiple courtyards creates a double facade in all the rooms – one facing the private courtyard, the other facing the shared courtyard – capitalising on the views towards two ends of the site: the mountain and the valley.

The overall envelope of the live/work clusters presents itself as three 'peaks' that contain the typological imprint of the Hakka/Tulou house. Binding these peaks is the gently undulating public ground, opening up vistas towards the valley of the site and also framing the needle-mountains of Guizhou from the valley. This act of framing the landscape also occurs at multiple levels – from the public ground to the shared courtyards to the double facades of the rooms – and is akin to the landscape scroll paintings of the Song Dynasty. In these paintings, the mountains are presented from a succession of viewpoints, captured as parts and yet presented as wholes.

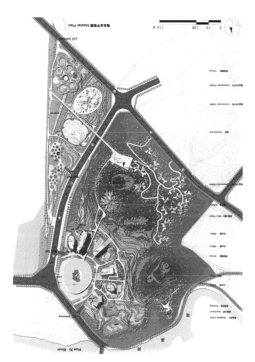

HX Urban Centre Masterplan, Guizhou, China

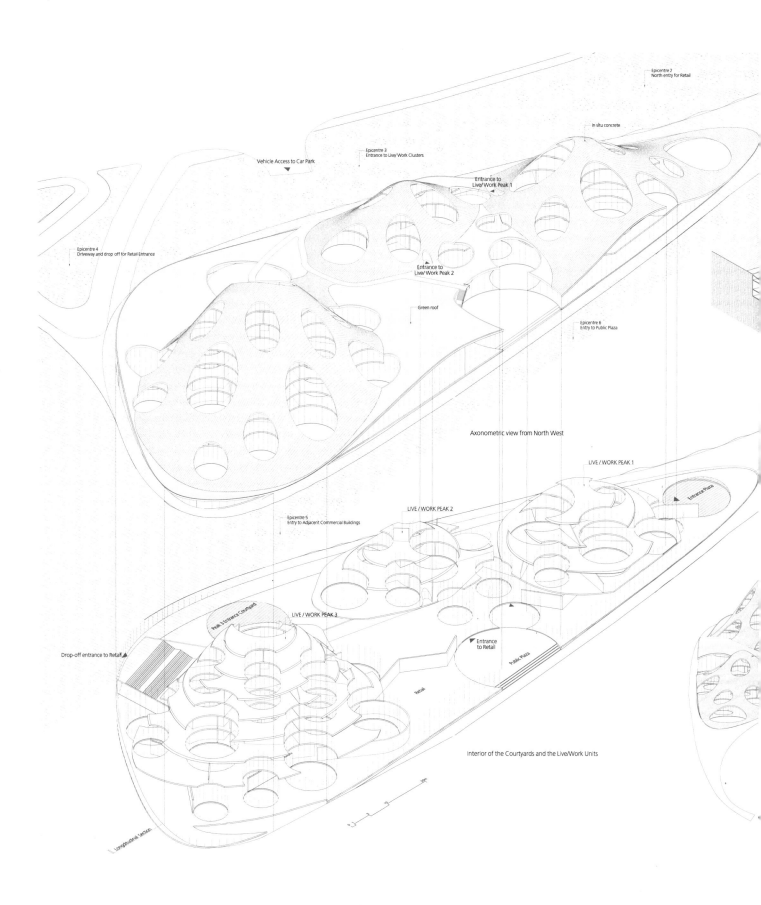

Epicentre 2
North entry for Retail

In situ concrete

Vehicle Access to Car Park

Epicentre 3
Entrance to Live/ Work Clusters

Entrance to
Live/ Work Peak 1

Epicentre 4
Driveway and drop off for Retail Entrance

Entrance to
Live/ Work Peak 2

Green roof

Epicentre 6
Entry to Public Plaza

Axonometric view from North West

LIVE / WORK PEAK 1

Epicentre 5
Entry to Adjacent Commercial Buildings

LIVE / WORK PEAK 2

Entrance Plaza

LIVE / WORK PEAK 3

Peak 3 Entrance Courtyard

Entrance
to Retail

Drop-off entrance to Retail

Public Plaza

Retail

Interior of the Courtyards and the Live/Work Units

Longitudinal Section

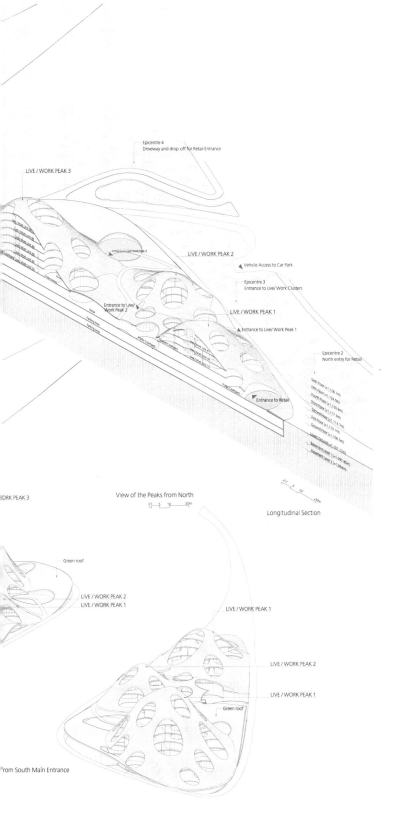

Epicentre 4
Driveway and drop off for Retail Entrance

LIVE / WORK PEAK 3

LIVE / WORK PEAK 2

Entrance to Live/ Work Peak 3

◄ Vehicle Access to Car Park

Epicentre 3
Entrance to Live/ Work Clusters

Entrance to Live/
Work Peak 2

LIVE / WORK PEAK 1

◄ Entrance to Live/ Work Peak 1

Epicentre 2
North entry for Retail

Sixth Floor (+128.1m)
Fifth Floor (+124.6m)
Fourth Floor (+120.9m)
Third Floor (+117.3m)
Second Floor (+113.7m)
First Floor (+110.1m)
Ground Floor (+106.5m)
Lower Ground (+101.1/120)
Basement Level 1 (+097.85m)
Basement Level 2 (+098m)

Entrance to Retail

WORK PEAK 3

View of the Peaks from North
01 5 10   20m

Longitudinal Section

Green roof

LIVE / WORK PEAK 2
LIVE / WORK PEAK 1

LIVE / WORK PEAK 1

LIVE / WORK PEAK 2

LIVE / WORK PEAK 1

Green roof

from South Main Entrance

Guo-Xi, Early Spring, hanging scroll. Ink on silk, 1702 (above left)
Hakka/ Tulou house (above right)

Type change: the typal imprint of the circular courtyard house transformed into
a clustered courtyards organisation with differing degrees of privacy

Matrix of differentiation:
clustering of circular courtyards to
varying heights

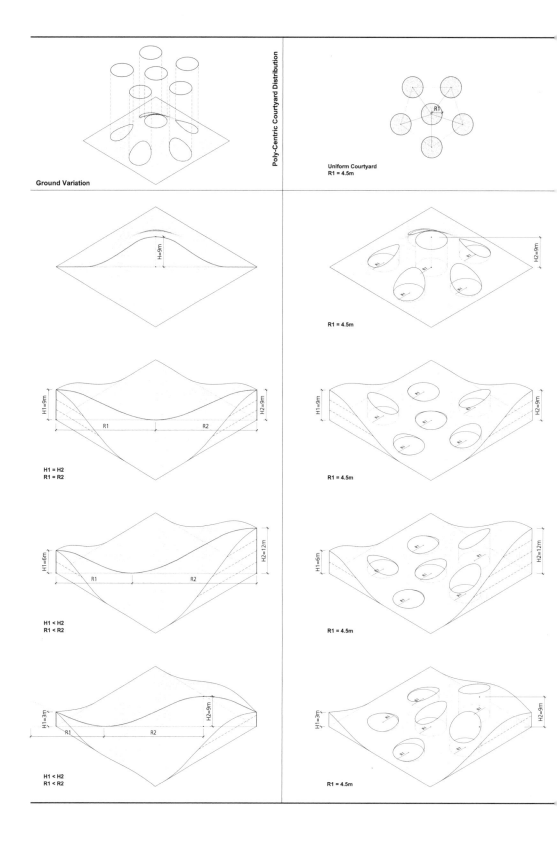

Poly-Centric Courtyard Distribution

Ground Variation

Uniform Courtyard
R1 = 4.5m

H=9m

R1 = 4.5m

H1 = 9m
H2 = 9m
R1
R2
H1 = H2
R1 = R2

R1 = 4.5m

H1=6m
H2=12m
R1
R2
H1 < H2
R1 < R2

R1 = 4.5m

H1=3m
H2=9m
R1
R2
H1 < H2
R1 < R2

R1 = 4.5m

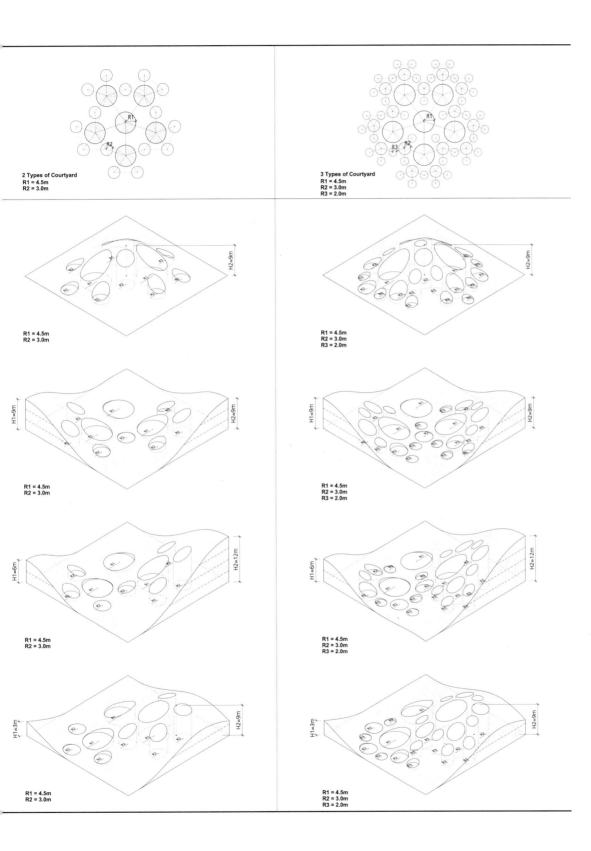

2 Types of Courtyard
R1 = 4.5m
R2 = 3.0m

3 Types of Courtyard
R1 = 4.5m
R2 = 3.0m
R3 = 2.0m

R1 = 4.5m
R2 = 3.0m

R1 = 4.5m
R2 = 3.0m
R3 = 2.0m

R1 = 4.5m
R2 = 3.0m

R1 = 4.5m
R2 = 3.0m
R3 = 2.0m

R1 = 4.5m
R2 = 3.0m

R1 = 4.5m
R2 = 3.0m
R3 = 2.0m

R1 = 4.5m
R2 = 3.0m

R1 = 4.5m
R2 = 3.0m
R3 = 2.0m

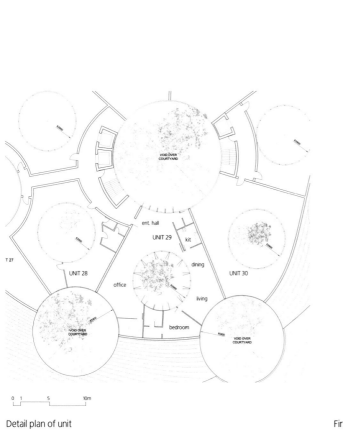

VOID OVER
COURTYARD

ent. hall

UNIT 29   kit

dining

office   UNIT 30

living

UNIT 28

bedroom

T 27

VOID OVER
COURTYARD

VOID OVER
COURTYARD

0 1   5   10m

Detail plan of unit

UNIT 3

UNIT 5   UNIT 4

UNIT 6   UNIT 7

0 1 5   10   20   50m

First floor plan

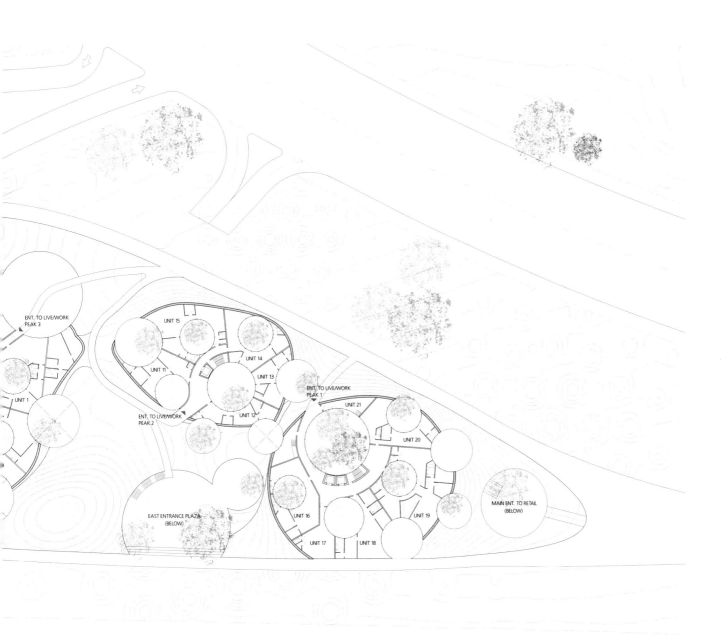

ENT. TO LIVE/WORK
PEAK 3

UNIT 15

UNIT 11

UNIT 1

UNIT 14

UNIT 13

ENT. TO LIVE/WORK
PEAK 2

ENT. TO LIVE/WORK
PEAK 1

UNIT 21

UNIT 12

UNIT 20

MAIN ENT. TO RETAIL
(BELOW)

EAST ENTRANCE PLAZA
(BELOW)

UNIT 16

UNIT 19

UNIT 17

UNIT 18

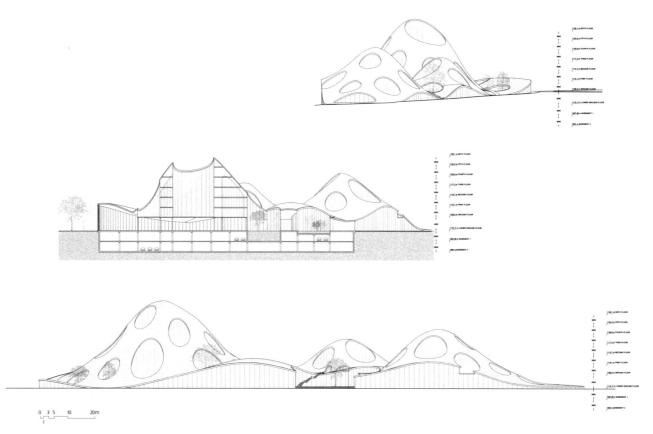

Section and elevations

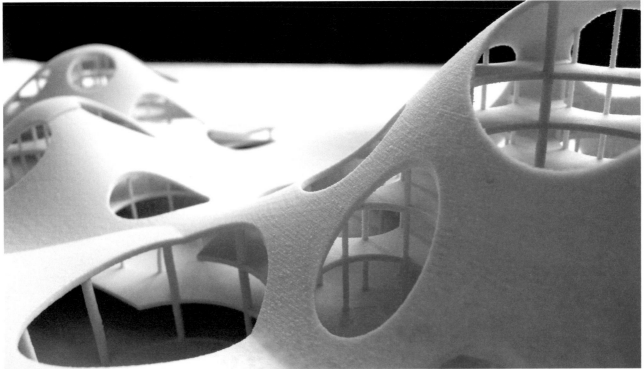

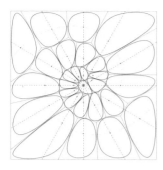

BOHÁCKY RESIDENTIAL MASTERPLAN
2009-ONGOING, BRATISLAVA, SLOVAKIA

COMPETITION 1ST PRIZE
Construction expected to begin in January 2011

At first this competition to 'masterplan' a residential development made up of villas seemed antithetical to our idea of the city. But not quite. We took the opportunity to rethink what constitutes 'infrastructure' in the form of boundaries that promote differences and enable them to co-exist. In the city, this will take the form of the plot, surrounded and nourished by infrastructure of mobility.

MASTERPLAN
Today's so-called 'luxury' housing development is confronted by two paradoxical ambitions: creating a sense of exclusivity for each villa and maximising the land for a profitable development. Often such developments end up being highly congested – despite a relatively average FAR – and incoherent, as each villa competes to be more exotic than the other.

The desire for 'exclusivity' in the context of private landed housing can also be thought of as the desire for privacy – to be away from the city, to be close to, enclosed by, nature. The ultimate form of private housing is perhaps like a retreat in a clearing in the middle of a forest.

To achieve this sense of privacy and isolation, we imagine the site first as a forest, from which clearings are made for the individual villas. These 'clearings' define the individual plots as enclosed outdoor rooms. A sense of privacy and exclusivity is achieved by having clear plot edges: hedges or manicured trees form the walls for these outdoor rooms. The use of hedges as an architectural feature on a large scale creates a visible coherent overall form. The undulating hedge is the primary design element of the masterplan. It seeks to bring together all the villas (which are designed by various architects) under one defining landscape element. Unlike hard boundaries such as brick walls and metal fences, the hedge offers a strategy for demarcation and security that is more natural, sustainable and can be seen as an extension of the natural environment of the site.

Different ideas of luxury: Jumeirah palm island and unknown dwelling in forest

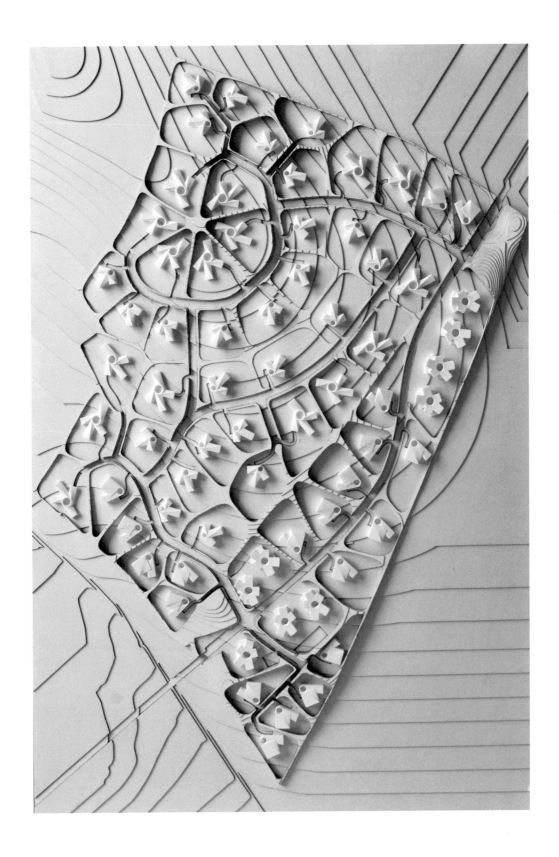

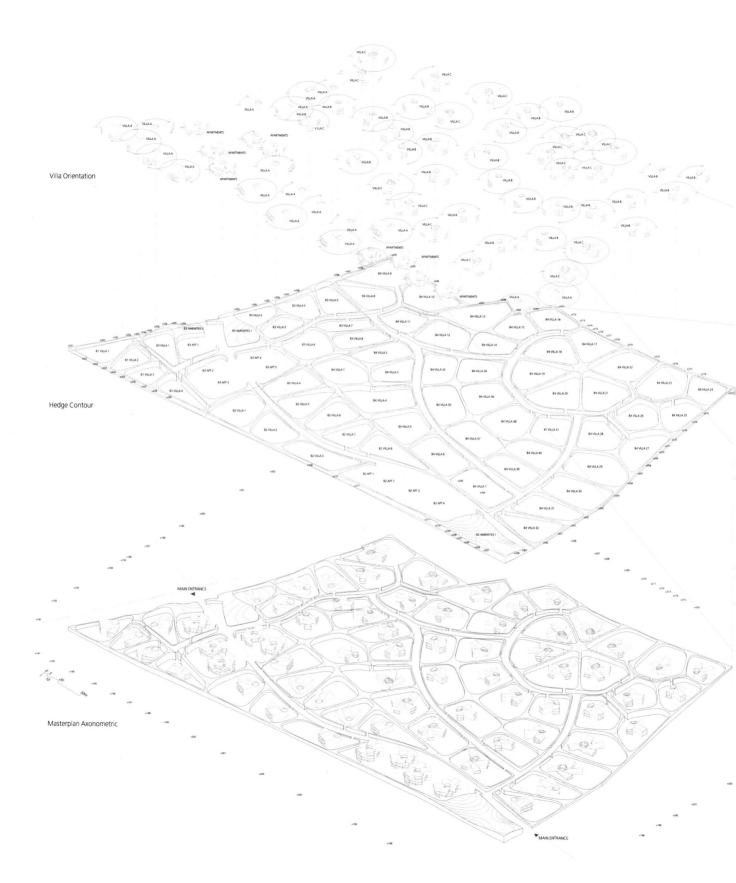

Villa Orientation

Hedge Contour

Masterplan Axonometric

MAIN ENTRANCE

MAIN ENTRANCE

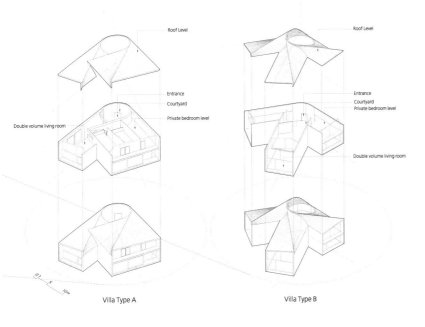

Roof Level

Entrance
Courtyard
Private bedroom level

Double volume living room

Villa Type A

Roof Level

Entrance
Courtyard
Private bedroom level

Double volume living room

Villa Type B

0 1   5   10m

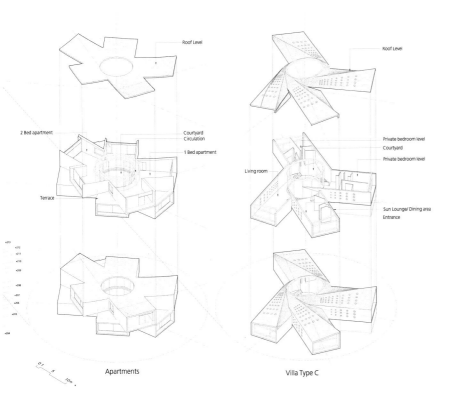

Roof Level

2 Bed apartment

Courtyard
Circulation

1 Bed apartment

Terrace

Apartments

Roof Level

Private bedroom level
Courtyard
Private bedroom level

Living room

Sun Lounge/ Dining area
Entrance

Villa Type C

0 1   5   10m

The hedges as a singular and complete artefact acts as an enabling 'infrastructure' that allows each plot to be an autonomous site for the villas created by other architects.

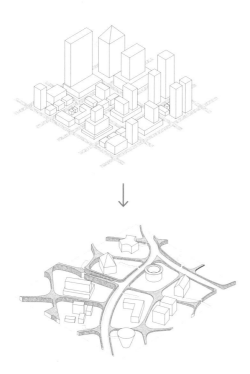

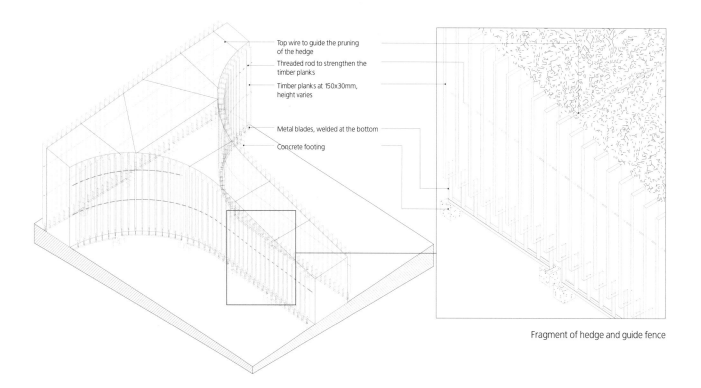

Top wire to guide the pruning of the hedge

Threaded rod to strengthen the timber planks

Timber planks at 150x30mm, height varies

Metal blades, welded at the bottom

Concrete footing

Fragment of hedge and guide fence

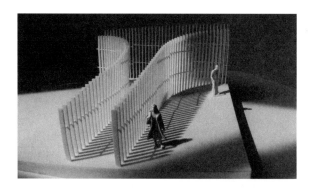

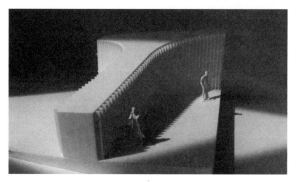

The guide fence is made up of two layers of timber planks that will guide and define the growth of the hedge. The first phase will see the construction of the timber fence that will demarcate all the various plots of the development and the overall envelope of the hedge. The subsequent phase will see the planting of the hedges.

Compared to bricks the hedge is a more natural and cost-effective solution and the timber fence can be sourced locally and can be recycled. The durability of the hedge also far exceeds that of a brick wall construction. We considered two species for the planting: one is evergreen and the other a vertical climber. Evergreen provides shelter and privacy year round, but requires regular pruning. Climbers grow at a faster rate compared to evergreens, and can still form the required hedge design envelope.

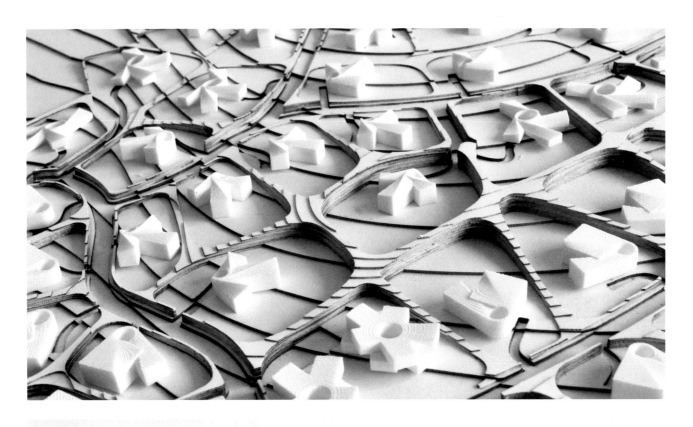

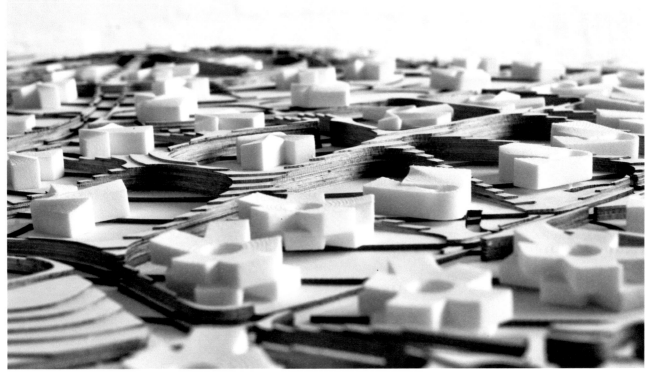

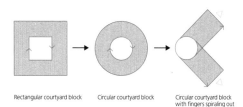

Rectangular courtyard block · Circular courtyard block · Circular courtyard block with fingers spiraling out

Rethinking the courtyard villa type

Increase in the number of fingers to allow different sizes

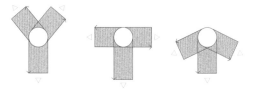

Orientation of the fingers to accommodate the topography and views

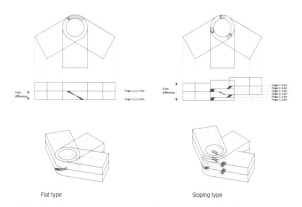

Flat type · Sloping type

Raising the fingers to accommodate the topography of the site

VILLA

The desire for difference in high-end developments often results in an exotic display of incoherent architectural styles. The challenge for the masterplan is to produce diversity while ensuring overall coherence. To achieve this, we propose to use the courtyard house as the common housing typology.

The courtyard house stands as a type that has persisted through the ages and across cultures. It is specific in its spatial relationships rather than its external form. Where the plot is envisioned as an outdoor room, the courtyard will be the semi-outdoor room on a more intimate scale.

Instead of rectangular courtyards, a circular courtyard offers a smoother circulation and spatial transition around its circumference. This type is further transformed into a spiralling courtyard type with fingers spinning off the circumference, adapting to the varying slopes of the site. These fingers create rooms orientated towards an outdoor view, framing the open spaces of the plot.

TYPOLOGICAL GRAMMAR FOR THE MASTERPLAN

The spiralling courtyards can be further developed into villas of varying sizes, allowing different interpretations of this master-plan. Thus the use of the courtyard type provides a typological grammar that enables different architects to speak the same language for a coherent development.

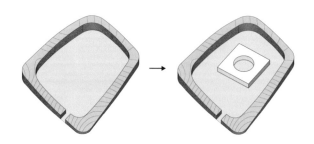

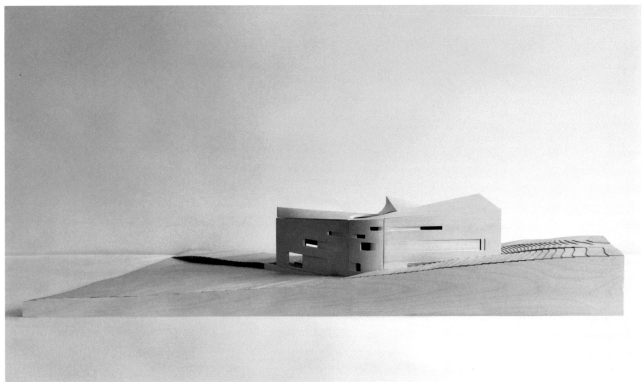

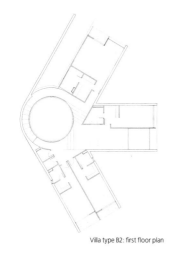

Villa type B2: first floor plan

Villa type B1: first floor plan

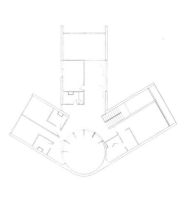

Villa type B3: first floor plan

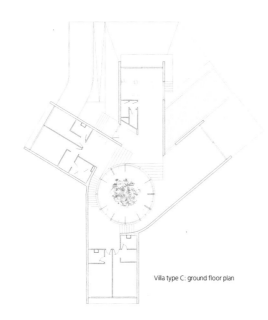

Villa type C: ground floor plan

Villa type A1: first floor plan

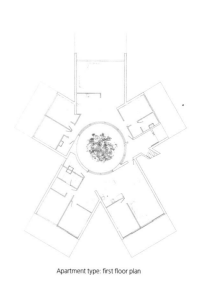

Apartment type: first floor plan

0 1 3 5   10m

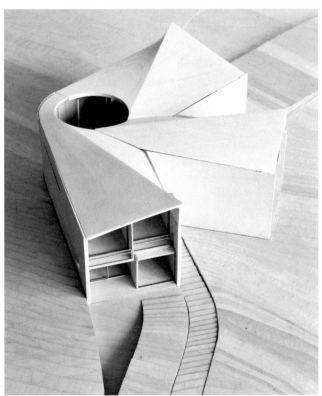

THE PRACTICE OF CONJECTURES AS PROJECT

Laurence Liauw

Although founded as a practice only three years ago, Serie's principals, Chris Lee and Kapil Gupta, have been practising together since 2002. Evolving from the AA's Diploma Unit 6, which Lee led (with Sam Jacoby), Serie's theoretical origination follows an established AA tradition of the unit master-practitioner model of research (in)forming practice in parallel, recalling the heyday of the 1970s when both Koolhaas and Tschumi were teaching at the AA before taking divergent career paths. [1] The question that needs to be asked is whether such a model is able to critically carry forward a project that began in academia, through the field of practice, creating new value which can be fed back into the disciplinary theory of architecture. This was one of the missions of nineteenth-century architectural thinkers and pioneering typologists such as J. N. L. Durand who imagined the profession as an academic discipline. [2] In the recent work of Serie, one sees the potential for this cross-fertilisation at a time when young contemporary practices seem to have abandoned disciplinary discourse.

One of the distinguishing characteristic traits of Serie as a practice is that it chooses to operate in three separate continents without attempting or succumbing to any contextual identity. Practising globally forces them to search for a theoretical consistency that enables coherent yet differentiated architectures. [3] This condition of global practice that distorts culture, time and space, drives Serie's determination to bring systemic typological ideas to different locales and innovate through serial differentiation and local adaptation. It is made apparent in their grids (facade) / vaults (ceiling) / circles (plan) taxonomy of projects, which are simultaneously classification and design technique. Building globally and operating within a smooth domain of idea-types, with variations on designs, it is the field (India and China as drivers for urbanisation and

1   On the work of Diploma 6, see Christopher Lee and Sam Jacoby, eds., *Typological Formations: Renewable Building Types and the City* (AA Publications, 2007). On the AA master-practitioner model, see Brett Steele and Francisco Gonzalez de Canales, eds., *First Works: Emerging Architectural Experimentation of the 1960s & 1970s* (AA Publications, 2009) 192–95.

2   J. N. L. Durand's influence on architectural discipline was at its peak when he taught at the Ecole Polytechnique in 1795, publishing two seminal texts, *Recueil et parallèle des edifices de tous genres, anciens et modernes,* 1801 and *Précis of the Lectures on Architecture,* 1805.

3   For a discussion of these issues in practice, see an interview with FOA's Alejandro Zaera-Polo by Guy Zucker (*32BNY* magazine, Issue 5/6, 2004).

architectural change) that generates new knowledge for Serie in London and Mumbai. This is opposite to practices that tend to colonise through established style, professional experience and sheer size. The city thus becomes Serie's site and material of architectural knowledge, forming a multi-scalar and transnational practice.

Both Lee and Gupta belong to and have since transcended a 90s generation of AA-educated architects well versed in iterative techniques and generative processes. In their evolving practice they have translated these skills into explorations of architecture's deep structure and a serial approach to materialising projects through type, as Lee puts it: 'to work typologically is to work in series… to surpass both idea and deep structure through differentiation'.[4] The last generation of emergent practices, such as FOA, UN Studio and Reiser+Umemoto, tactically adopted taxonomical, populational or indexical 'species' as their organisation models for practice.[5] Serie have extended these iterative non-linear methods, and deployed serialised types (instead of prototypes) embedded with both idea and conflict. Types are then critically subjected to systemic transformation, generating new spatial and structural configurations. Whilst both generations have moved away from theorising images and text towards theorising materialism and physical structures, Serie's practice has called for a return to spatial organisation as the primary activity of the architect.[6] From the 'deep plan'[7] towards 'deep structure',[8] striving for this coherence articulates the architectural qualities of Serie's project.

THEORY (OF TYPES)

Rooted in the belief that types mediate between architecture and city, idea and model, structure and space, Serie's theoretical underpinnings can be traced back to type as a discipline within architectural culture. Already widely discussed are Quatremère de Quincy's and J. N. L. Durand's different conceptions of type as idea and model in architecture (especially Quatremère's idea that must serve as the rule to the model).[9] Both are present in Serie's thinking. Reference can also be made to Sylvia Lavin's thesis on Quatremère's transformation of type as an operative system,[10] and Rafael Moneo's position on typology[11] where type is an 'inherent structure and formal order that allows architectural objects to be grouped together, distinguished and repeated; whereby architecture is not only described by types but also produced through them'. Previous thinkers such as Goethe had also posited type as abstract formative principle.[12] These theoretical views support the abstraction of type through diagramming – as Jeffrey Kipnis has pointed out.[13] Type's organisational function is captured in the diagram, whether static, pliant or associative. Not to be confused with, but nevertheless emerging from the diagrammatic generation of 90s architecture typified by generative design processes as modes of production.

Serie's use of type as proliferating device rather than one of replication and contextualisation is a clear break from the previous generation of typologists of the past 30 years.[14] Repetition and differentiation as formulated by Deleuze[15] parallel 'working in series' as a real system of always-differential relations of repetitive incremental change that create actual differentiated spaces, times and sensations. Durand's typologi-

4   Christopher Lee and Sam Jacoby, op. cit., 147.
5   FOA, UN Studio and Reiser + Umemoto's practice manifestos can be found in *Phylogenesis* (Actar, 2003), *Atlas of Novel Tectonics* (Princeton Architectural Press, 2006) and *UN Studios: Design Models - Architecture, Urbanism Infrastructure* (Rizzoli, 2006).
6   Recent conversations between the author and Chris Lee in London, Beijing, Hong Kong, 2008–10.
7   The Deep Plan as an emergent concept of dynamic large-scale organisational structures has been promoted by UN Studio for a number of years, most recently in an essay 'Deep Plan' for the publication *Large Scale Metropolises* (Centre Pompidou, 2009), 78–79.
8   Deep Structure has been defined by Chris Lee as 'that which gives rise to the organisation of space and form' in conversation with the author, 2010. This is intended to be a critique of other organisations that focus on surface and form only.

9   For a discussion of these distinctions of idea and model see essays in Christopher Lee and Sam Jacoby, op. cit., 136–56.
10   See Sylvia Lavin, *Quatremère de Quincy and the Invention of a Modern Language of Architecture* (MIT Press, 1992) 86–100.
11   See Rafael Moneo, 'On Typology', in *Rafael Moneo 1967-2004* (El Croquis, 2004).
12   Reference made by Sanford Kwinter to Goethe's understanding of type in 'Who's Afraid of Formalism', in *Phylogenesis* (Actar, 2003), 96–99.
13   See Jeff Kipnis, 'Reoriginating Diagrams', in *Peter Eisenman: Feints* (Skira, 2006).
14   Reference can be made to the previous generation of typologists active in the 1960s and 1970s, including Giulio Carlo Argan, Aldo Rossi, Alan Colquhoun, Rob Krier, Colin Rowe and Tony Vidler.
15   See Gilles Deleuze, *Difference and Repetition* (Columbia University Press 1994).

cal models' deep structure diagrams and Quatremère's idea as socio-cultural critique support the reflexive formulation of type that Serie's architecture promotes. The discourse of type is also elevated to the level of the city, recalling Aldo Rossi's early definition of types as urban structure and permanences that were free from programmatic change.[16] Rossi's freedom *of* types is a question of form, whereas Rem Koolhaas' freedom *from* types is a question of ideology.[17] Serie sits comfortably between these two positions, addressing both in their own work. Le Corbusier also made a theoretical shift from prototypes (object-types) to models early in his career, with implications for organisational structures and the production of buildings. Serie's discourse navigates around most of these theoretical aspects in its formulation of type as the central architectural thesis on their project for the city. These theoretical claims and alignments are partially revealed by their project's ambition – aiming for both the strategic and tactical in their method, encapsulating both idea and model in their projective types. As Serie's Lee puts it, 'iteratively transformed types reveal new potentials of spatial organisation that surpass precedent types whilst retaining shared traits … the deep structure of type has the architectural ability to organise space and material, which other disciplines cannot.'[18] A recent shift in Lee's teaching from the question of 'type and the urban plan' to 'type and the city', with the claim that the city should be understood as an architectural project through its dominant type, underlines Serie's commitment to architectural knowledge emerging from the city. Type's performative qualities and instrumentality at different scales are central to their theoretical apparatus. Variations of type as Serie sees them go beyond the formal and programmatic, but embody a (historically) charged discourse of where architecture comes from and where it is going.

FROM FIELD TO DISCIPLINE

Serie's work in the field of practice attempts to locate a position within the discipline of architectural knowledge in three ways. Firstly, the claim that *architecture as a material practice* can become projective, instrumental and operative. Within the field there has been a shift from discursive practices of the 60s and 70s to material practices of the 90s onwards. Problematising building matter has replaced anti-disciplinary discourse, but now to the extent that materialism without argument or agenda dominates architectural practice today. Deployment of technological driven design instruments for Serie is present in their design method, but not an end in itself. The return to projects is more urgent than developing procedural tools. The undertaking of a building project as the basis for the discovery and invention of architecture knowledge rather than through written theory is their modus operandi as a disciplinary practice.[19] Secondly, their ambition that *architecture can serve as political agency* relies on architectural types to exert influence and mediate conflicting differences that typify the contemporary life of cities.[20] This projective approach of architecture as an agent of urban change underlines the project of the city through type as both idea (why) and model (how) for the city.[21] Type for Serie is a medium to think about and affect cities, so that architecture's own internal discourse is externalised by practices that contest and negotiate economic, cultural, political and environmental differences. Typal practice hence becomes the strategic mediation and opportunism within the field, and in doing so politicises the discipline. Thirdly, *architecture's contemporary global practice* has superseded the modern architectural office in that location of ideas, types and operations are no longer stable or predictable.[22] Contemporary global practice evolves as new types emerge

16 See Aldo Rossi's elaboration on type and urban structure in his seminal book *Architecture and the City* (MIT Press, 1984).
17 Interview with Rem Koolhaas by Alejandro Zaera-Polo on 'Finding Freedoms' alluded to freedom from types, which was subsequently included in Koolhaas' list of freedoms in later writings, 'OMA Rem Koolhaas 1987–1993' (*El Croquis*, 1994), 6–31.
18 Recent conversations between the author and Chris Lee in London, Beijing, Hong Kong, 2007–10.
19 See Brett Steele, 'Last Laughs and Plenty to Say', op. cit., 6–20.
20 Bruno Latour discusses political agency in his writings, especially his actor-network theory, claiming that objects too have agency. See publications *Politics of Nature: How to Bring the Sciences into Democracy* (Harvard University Press, 2004) and *Reassembling the Social: An Introduction to Actor-Network-Theory* (Oxford University Press, 2005).
21 Conversations with Serie principals at a lecture in Hong Kong University in 2009.
22 Conversations between the author and Enrique Walker about the difference in career and types of architect offices of Rem Koolhaas and Bernard Tschumi, distinguishing between the contemporary office and modern office (Beijing, 2010).

and the idea of the city changes the forms of architectural engagement and production. Generic architectural knowledge and ideas are now transmitted to foreign places requiring a specific architectural response and typological adaptation. The opportunity for Serie to build in rapidly urbanising India and China puts to the test the practice and theory of architecture beyond mere tooling, and instead, through the actualisation of projects, generates new architectural knowledge and material culture. For Serie, the trajectory and evolution of their practice through type strives to be consistent, differential and critical. This is achieved primarily through the project of the city, as a critical practice of conjecture and serial explorations.

CRITICAL PROJECTION

AA director Brett Steele has examined how critical architects' first works have the ability to 'reconnect two remote forms of knowledge – theory and practice'. [23] In Serie's first built project, Blue Frog (although not at the scale of an entire building), one sees their theoretical coherence materialised in the organisation of space and form. This deep structure organisation is later to be recalled and differentiated in their Bohácky masterplan and recent Indian projects. Practice is therefore no longer a demonstration of theoretical positions, but itself essential for new theory to emerge. Typology for Serie, is not merely the practice of classifications but instrumental to practice through an operative theory of type. The institutionalised separation of practice and theory in contemporary practice begs the question of when architecture knowledge will come out of hiding from academia. [24] Holding out through the singular academic development of speculative prototypes often prevents advanced theoretical domains from crossing over into practice. This is a challenge Serie is clearly trying to address in both their theory and practice in a disciplinary manner. Sylvia Lavin has lamented that there is 'no contemporary theory of practice, just shoptalk about buildings'. [25] Lavin continues to note the current 'historical shift of resistant theoretical architects into professional practice, spurred on by the global building boom.

Architects must return to building as a matter of principle not by accident or anecdote, indicating that architecture is ready to emerge from its hideout'. This call to arms by contemporary practitioners such as Serie is no less than a manifesto for the conceptualisation of architecture, production of buildings and invention of theory, through a return to conjectural projects as a complete act of architecture.

---

23 See Brett Steele and Francisco Gonzalez de Canales, op. cit.
24 The hide-and-seek relationship between academia and practice is discussed in an essay by Sylvia Lavin, 'Practice makes perfect', *Hunch* 11 (Rotterdam: Winter 2006/7), 106–13.
25 Ibid.

DEEP STRUCTURE 3

FACADE / GRIDS

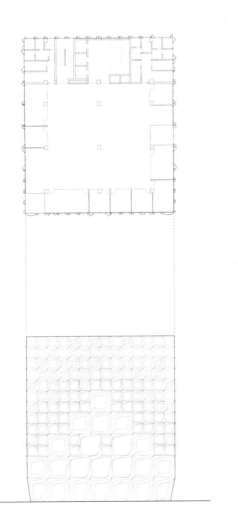

V Office, Mumbai

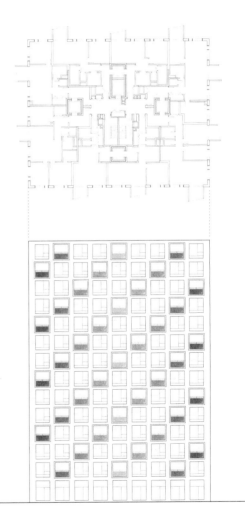

Ružinov Middle Income Housing, Bratislava

V OFFICE
2007, MUMBAI, INDIA

In Mumbai today, the proliferation of curtain walls in fast paced, speculative office buildings has reduced the role of the architect to a mere elevation dresser. This phenomenon is blanketing the city with an endless uninspired combination of aluminium frames and glazing; the domain of the architect's role confined to a 200mm depth.

Resisting this tendency, our proposal aims to reinterpret the various components that make up an elevation whilst maintaining the maximum floor area that can be generated by building to the extent of the site boundary. The proposal imagines a modulated facade, made up of nine modules, that performs as a series of loggias, storage spaces, sun-shades and window-cabins all moulded into one. The size of openings on the facade is modulated by the amount of dilation of each of the modules which responds to the position of the facade in relation to the sun and also the programme within. The depth of the facade is thus thickened to 2m to enable balconies, break-out spaces, private cabins and tiered-seating for an auditorium. This thickening enables the facade to act more as an envelope that draws a closer relation between the external environment and the internal organisation of programme.

As a result, the speculative office block does not necessarily result in the ubiquitous open plan office. The use of the facade/grids as a deep structure induces a hierarchical difference in plan, enabling the various communal rooms to aggregate around a more speculative open plan.

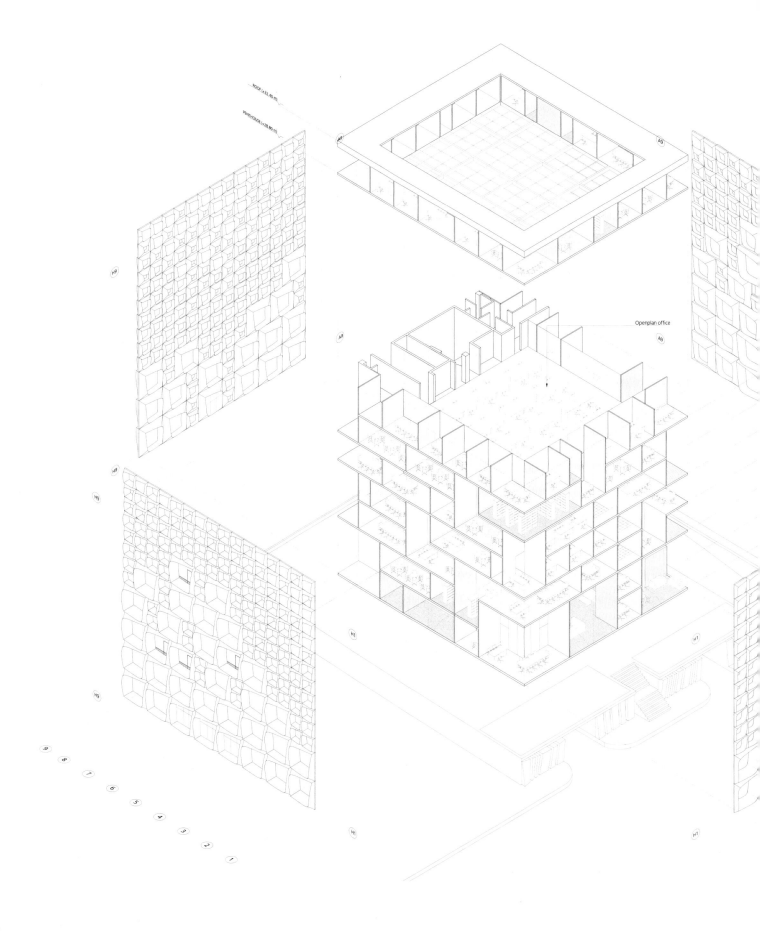

ROOF (+32.40 m)

PENTHOUSE (+28.80 m)

Openplan office

A9

A9

A9

A9

H9

H9

H9

H9

H1

H1

H1

H1

9 8 7 6 5 4 3 2 1

The modulated facade performs as a series of loggias, storage spaces, sun-shades and window-cabins all moulded into one. This thickening enables the facade to act more as an envelope that draws a closer relation between the external environment and the internal organisation of programme.

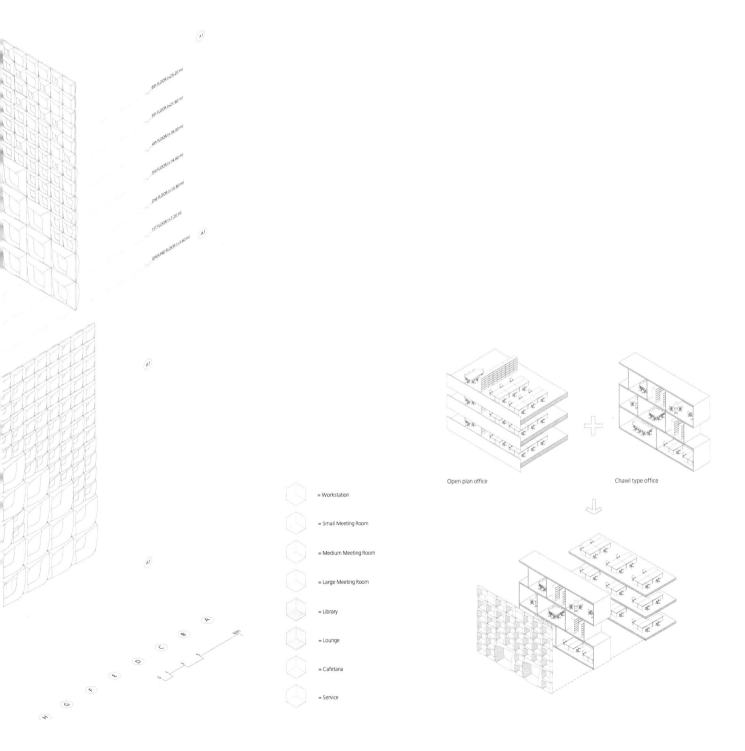

6th FLOOR (+25.20 m)

5th FLOOR (+21.60 m)

4th FLOOR (+18.00 m)

3rd FLOOR (+14.40 m)

2nd FLOOR (+10.80 m)

1ST FLOOR (+7.20 m)

GROUND FLOOR (+3.60 m)

= Workstation

= Small Meeting Room

= Medium Meeting Room

= Large Meeting Room

= Library

= Lounge

= Cafetaria

= Service

Open plan office

Chawl type office

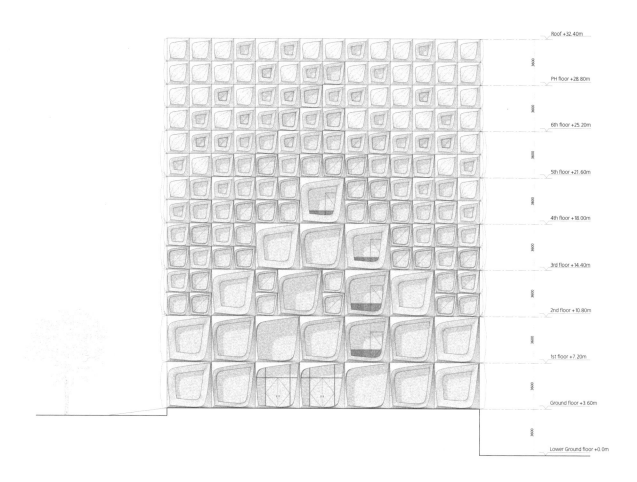

Roof +32.40m

3600

PH floor +28.80m

3600

6th floor +25.20m

3600

5th floor +21.60m

3600

4th floor +18.00m

3600

3rd floor +14.40m

3600

2nd floor +10.80m

3600

1st floor +7.20m

3600

Ground floor +3.60m

3600

Lower Ground floor +0.0m

0 1   3   5   10m

Elevation

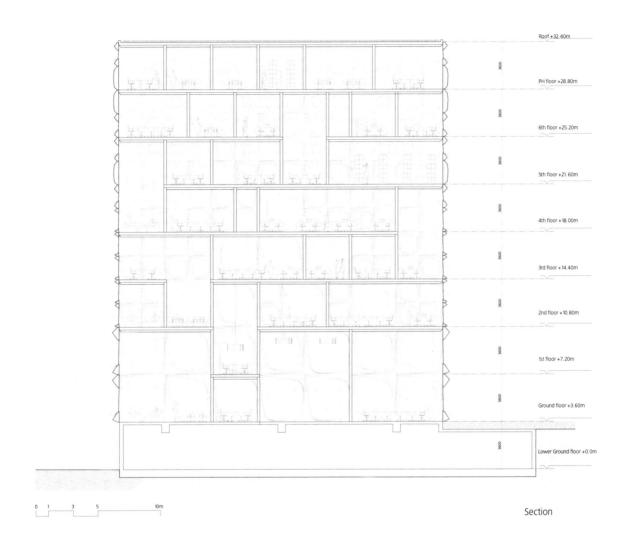

Roof +32.40m

PH floor +28.80m

6th floor +25.20m

5th floor +21.60m

4th floor +18.00m

3rd floor +14.40m

2nd floor +10.80m

1st floor +7.20m

Ground floor +3.60m

Lower Ground floor +0.0m

0 1   3   5   10m

Section

1. Study model of the facade module
2,3. Mock-up of mesh structure of module
4. Mock-up after being sprayed with concrete

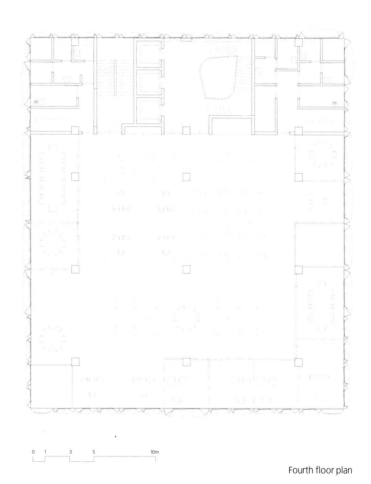

0   1   3   5   10m

Fourth floor plan

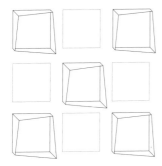

RUŽINOV MIDDLE INCOME HOUSING
2009-ONGOING, BRATISLAVA, SLOVAKIA

COMPETITION 1ST PRIZE
Construction expected to begin in March 2011

This high-density, middle income housing, to be built on a tight budget, posed two fundamental and enduring problems of mass housing: how can monotony be avoided or reduced as the result of the need for repetition that enables efficient and economical construction and how can a balance be struck between uniformity and variety, communal decorum and individual expression?

The project site lies on the southwest corner of the intersection of two busy thoroughfares, Ružinovská and Bajkalská and slopes down towards Lake Strkovecke. The brief stipulates a high FAR of 4.5 and calls for the provision of 440 units of apartments with a relatively low construction budget. Our response was to distribute the required numbers of apartments into a family of towers of varying heights – 29, 19 and 12 storeys – with the shortest closest to the lake and the tallest furthest from it. The towers are clustered together loosely around a central entrance and communal space. The tower is a simple extrusion of a rectangular plan with a 3.3m grid to allow effective subdivision of flats, rooms and openings.

Continuing the strategies of the V Office, the project utilises the gridded facade as the deep structure to create a thickened and modulated facade out of rooms. Here, loggias of different depth create a semi-outdoor room, laid out on a rhythm of a 2:1 bay and undulating inwards and outwards to imply a second surface that is curvaceous in contrast to the orthogonal facade. The placement of the loggias in this configuration also draws the living rooms along the facade diagonally, thus disabling the direct stacking of living rooms or identical units type one above another. In turn, through the facade, we generated 56 unique apartment layouts (with minimal increase in cost of construction). Thus the deep structure of the gridded facade is utilised to confront two current problems. The first denies the rampant random facades that typify mass housing of late, where the conspicuous expression of different apartment units on the facade, expressed as singular instances (and as a celebration of individuality) denies any sense of order and coherence and negates the very notion of collective housing. Following on from this, the second response is to provide for a high degree of differentiation in apartment layouts where these differences cohere into a collective whole that is ordered and legible.

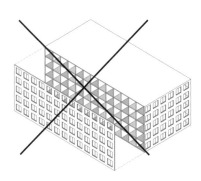

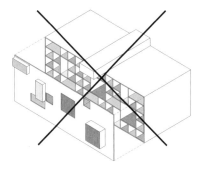

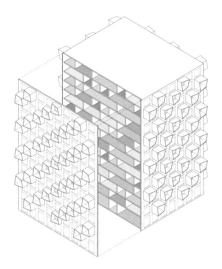

Ordered facade:
undifferentiated repetition of apartment units

Random, expressive and disordered facade:
differentiated apartment units

Individual difference coheres into an ordered whole:
differentiated apartment units regulated by an
overall order

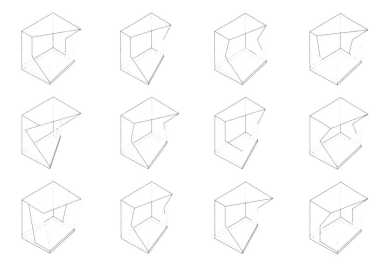

Balcony variation

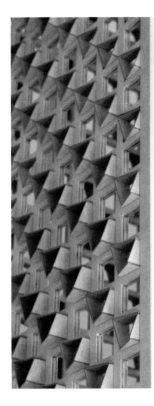

MAIN
ENTRANCE

PEDESTRIAN PATH /
FIRE ACCESS
ROUTE

INGRESS/EGRESS
TO CARPARK

TOWER A
RETAIL ENT.
(BELOW)

EAST
ENTRANCE

FL +140.15M
SL +139.85M

TOWER A
RESIDENTIAL
ENTRANCE

FL +140.15M
SL +139.85M

TOWER B
RESIDENTIAL
ENTRANCE

FL +140.15M
SL +139.85M

TOWER C
ENTRANCE
(BELOW)

PICNIC / BBQ
AREA

FL +140.5M
SL +140.7M

0 1   5   10   20m

Ground floor plan

148

BIOGRAPHY

SERIE ARCHITECTS

Serie Architects, founded in 2007, is based in London, Mumbai, Beijing and Chengdu. The practice's theoretical interest lies in the relationship between dominant types and the city. The practice works typologically – thinking and designing in series – and is committed to the projection of the cumulative intelligence of types into architectural projects. Serie was named as one of the ten visionary architects for the new decade by the Leading European Architects Forum. Serie is the *BD* Young Architect of the Year Runner-up 2008, and one of *ICON*'s 20 Essential Young International Architects. The works of Serie have been exhibited as a travelling solo exhibition in Hong Kong University Shanghai Architecture Gallery, Shanghai in 2009 and will culminate in a show at the Architectural Association in November 2010. The practice has completed, among others, the award-winning Blue Frog and The Tote. Current projects include Hangzhou Xin Tian Di Factory H in China, Ružinov Middle Income Housing and Boháčky Residential development in Bratislava.

CHRISTOPHER C. M. LEE

Christopher C. M. Lee is the co-founder and principal of Serie Architects. He graduated with the AA Diploma (Hons) and is the co-director of the Projective Cities Programme. He previously taught at the AA in Histories and Theories Studies (2009–10) and was a Unit Master in the Diploma School (Unit 6, 2004–09) and Intermediate School (Unit 2, 2002–04). He is pursuing his doctoral research at the Berlage Institute Rotterdam on the topic of the dominant type and the city.

KAPIL GUPTA

Kapil Gupta is the co-founder and principal of Serie Architects. He graduated with honors from Sir JJ School of Architecture, Mumbai in 1996 followed by postgraduate studies at the Architectural Association, London. He was a Director of the Urban Design Research Institute, Mumbai between 2003 and 2008.

WORKING IN SERIE

CONTRIBUTORS

Adarsh Akella
Advait Potnis
Ajay Sonar
Ali Asad
Amit Arya
Atish Rathod
Bolam Lee l Associate, Serie London
Dharmesh Thakker
Donny Prijatna
Hemant Purohit
Hong Che Yeow
Jeeseon Lim
Jin Kim
Joseph Halligan
Kevin Hung
Kunal Ghevaria
Leopold Lambert
Martin Jameson l Associate, Serie London
Max Von Werz
Mayank Ojha
Michelle Young
Naina Gupta
Niti Gourisaria
Patrick Usborne
Purva Jamdade
Renu Gupta
Santosh Thorat l Senior Architect, Serie Mumbai
Saurabh Biswas
Shamir Panchal
Simon Whittle
Stephie Sun Qin l Director, Serie Beijing
Sunil Thukrul
Suril Patel
Suruchi Agarwal
Tomas Ruis Osborne
Udayan Mazumdar
Vrinda Seksaria
Yael Gilad
Yicheng Pan
Yifan Liu l Director, Serie Chengdu

CREDITS

CEILING / VAULTS

01 THE TOTE
Use: Banqueting hall, restaurant, bar
Location: Mumbai, India
Total Area: 2500m^2
Design: Chris Lee and Kapil Gupta
Project Team: Yael Gilad, Dharmesh Thakker, Suril Patel, Purva Jamdade, Advait Potnis, Hemant Purohit, Vrinda Seksaria, Udayan Mazumdar, Adarsh Akella, Mayank Ojha, Atish Rathod
Design Phase: October 2006–September 2007
Construction Phase: December 2007–October 2009
Models: Jin Kim and Micro Models Beijing
Model Photography: Michelle Young
Structural Engineering: Facet Construction Engineering Pvt. Ltd
Mechanical and Electrical Engineering: AARK Consulting
Lighting Design: AWA Lighting Designers
Sound Design: Nexus Audio Video with Ole Christensen
Landscape Design: Apeiron Architects
Project Management: Masters Management Consultants
Metal Fabrication: Unique Concrete Technologies
Interior Contractors: Interex
Liaison Architects: Barai Architects and Engineers
Photography: Edmund Sumner and Fram Petit

02 MESWANI HOUSE
Use: Single family house
Location: Pavna Lake, India
Total Built Area: 1,500m^2
Design Team: Chris Lee, Kapil Gupta, Bolam Lee, Martin Jameson, Jin Kim, Shamir Panchal, Santosh Thorat, Suril Patel, Saurabh Biswas, Atish Rathod
Date: Concept Design April 2009
Total Built Area: 1,500m^2
Date: Concept Design April 2009
Model Photography: Michelle Young

03 XI'AN 2011 INTERNATIONAL HORTICULTURAL EXPO MASTERPLAN
Competition 2nd Prize
Use: Public building [exhibition/performance/greenhouse]
Location: Xi'an, China
Total Area: 24,000m^2
Design Team: Chris Lee, Kapil Gupta, Bolam Lee, Martin Jameson, Sun Qin
Client: 2011/ Xi'an International Horticultural Expo Organisation
Date: Competition Dec 2008 – Feb 2010
Models: Kevin Hung, Michelle Young and Joseph Halligan
Model Photography: Michelle Young

PLAN / CIRCLES

04 BLUE FROG ACOUSTIC LOUNGE & STUDIOS
Use: Bar, restaurant, performance space
Location: Mumbai, India
Total Area: 1,000m²
Design: Chris Lee and Kapil Gupta
Project Team: Tomas Ruis Osborne, Santosh Thorat, Purva Jamdade, Suril Patel,
Dharmesh Thakker, Niti Gourisaria, Vrinda Seksaria
Design to Completion: October 2006 – November 2007
Models: Jin Kim and Micro Models Beijing
Model Photography: Michelle Young
Acoustic Design: Munroe Acoustics (UK)
Lighting Design: AWA Lighting Designers
Project Management: Masters Management Consultants
General Contractor: Zigma Enterprises
Client: Blue Frog Media Pvt. Ltd
Photography: Fram Petit

05 XIN TIAN DI FACTORY H
Use: Adaptive re-use of factory to commercial and offices
Location: Hangzhou, China
Total Area: 8,040m²
Design Team: Chris Lee, Kapil Gupta, Bolam Lee, Martin Jameson, Sun Qin, Yifan
Liu, Kevin Hung, Amit Arya
Date: May 2010 – ongoing, construction expected January 2011
Models: Joseph Halligan and Michelle Young
Model Photography: Michelle Young

06 PARCEL 9, HX URBAN CENTRE
Use: Commercial, live/work, public space
Location: Guizhou, China
Total Area: 16,000m²
Design Team: Chris Lee, Kapil Gupta, Bolam Lee, Martin Jameson, Udayan
Mazumdar, Kevin Hung
Date: Concept design July – October 2008
Models: Jin Kim and Micro Models Beijing
Model Photography: Michelle Young

07 BOHÁCKY RESIDENTIAL DEVELOPMENT
Competition 1st Prize
Use: Single family house and masterplan
Location: Bratislava, Slovakia
Total Plot Area: 158,473m²
Total GBA: 37,621m²
Design Team: Chris Lee, Kapil Gupta, Bolam Lee, Martin Jameson
Date: Competition 1st Prize (December 2008), Phase 2 (January 2009– on-going)
Models: Joseph Halligan and Michelle Young
Model Photography: Michelle Young
Executive Architect: Architekti Bobek Javorka

FACADE / GRIDS

08 V OFFICE
Use: Office
Location: Mumbai, India.
Total Area: 6,500m²
Design Team: Chris Lee, Kapil Gupta, Santosh Thorat Advait Potnis, Hemant
Purohit, Udayan Mazumdar, Hong Che Yeow, Naina Gupta, Kunal Ghevaria, Ajay
Sonar, Tomas Ruis Osborne
Date: Design – February 2007, Completion – September 2007 (prototype stage)
Client: Verma Properties
Models: Yifan Liu and Michelle Young
Model Photography: Michelle Young

09 RUŽINOV MIDDLE INCOME HOUSING
Competition 1st Prize
Use: High-density middle income housing
Location: Bratislava, Slovakia
Total Plot Area: 9,702m²
Total GBA: 44,000m²
Design Team: Chris Lee, Bolam Lee, Martin Jameson, Jin Kim, Yifan Liu, Kevin
Hung, Michelle Young, Joseph Halligan
Date: July 2009 – ongoing, construction expected December 2010
Models: Michelle Young and Joseph Halligan
Model Photography: Michelle Young
Executive Architect: Siebert + Talaš, spol. s r.o.

COLOPHON

Working in Series
Christopher C. M. Lee and Kapil Gupta / Serie Architects

Managing Editor: Thomas Weaver
Publications Editor: Pamela Johnston
Art Director: Zak Kyes
Design: Bolam Lee
Editorial Assistant: Clare Barrett

Special thanks for their support to:
Yangkuo Enterprise Development Co. Ltd.,
3DD, Cavendish Imaging and Unit 22

Printed in Belgium by Cassochrome

ISBN 978-1-902902-98-2   EXAT ·

For a catalogue of AA Publications visit
www.aaschool.ac.uk/publications
or email publications@aaschool.ac.uk

AA Publications
36 Bedford Square
London WC1B 3ES

T + 44 (0)20 7887 4021
F + 44 (0)20 7414 0783